Silly Shakespeare for Students

I0530326

HAMLET

PAUL LEONARD MURRAY

with help from

WILLIAM SHAKESPEARE

Alphabet
PUBLISHING

ISBN: 978-1-956159-70-7 (paperback)
ISBN: 978-1-956159-71-4 (ebook)

Copyright 2024 by Paul Murray

All rights reserved. Our authors, editors, and designers work hard to develop original, high-quality content. Please respect their efforts and their rights under copyright law.

Do not copy, photocopy, or reproduce this book or any part of this book for use inside or outside the classroom, in commercial or non-commercial settings. It is also forbidden to copy, adapt, or reuse this book or any part of this book for use on websites, blogs, or third-party lesson-sharing websites.

For permission requests or discounts on class sets and bulk orders contact us at:

Alphabet Publishing
29 Milo Drive
Branford, CT 06405 USA

info@alphabetpublishingbooks.com
www.alphabetpublishingbooks.com

For performance rights, please contact Paul Murray at paulplaying@gmail.com

Interior Formatting and Cover Design by Melissa Williams Design

I dedicate this book to the following members of Belgrade English Language Youth Theatre, who, among other things, brought Silly Shakespeare Macbeth to life so wonderfully on the stage and inspired my further creations in this series. Thanks to you all!

Maša Alivojvodić
Maksimilijan Drenča
Tamara Grujić
Matija Mihić
Lena Milinković
Đorđe Radojević
Stanko Radojević
Nebojša Sofronijević
Lenka Stanišić
Katarina Stefanović
Nađa Vainomaa

The Story Behind Shakespeare's Hamlet

Imagine a play so powerful and timeless that it has captivated audiences for over 400 years. That's exactly what *Hamlet*, written by William Shakespeare, represents. First performed around 1600, this tragic play remains one of the most studied and celebrated works in literature. Let's dive into the history of *Hamlet*, explore its origins, and see why it continues to be so relevant today.

Origins of the Play

Hamlet is based on a legendary Danish prince whose story dates back to ancient Scandinavia. The earliest versions of the Hamlet legend come from Norse sagas and medieval stories. One of the primary sources for Shakespeare's *Hamlet* was a 16th-century play by a writer named Thomas Kyd, called *The Spanish Tragedy*. Kyd's play was a popular revenge tragedy, a genre where the hero seeks vengeance for a wrong. Shakespeare borrowed elements from this and other sources to create his own version.

Shakespeare's *Hamlet* was likely influenced by the works of earlier playwrights and storytellers, including the 12th-century Danish historian Saxo Grammaticus, *whose Gesta Danorum* (Deeds of the Danes) included a tale of a prince who sought revenge for his father's murder. Additionally, another important source was the *Histories Tragiques* by François de Belleforest, which also featured a story about Prince Hamlet.

The Plot

Hamlet is set in Denmark, a kingdom dealing with political unrest and personal tragedy. The play kicks off with the ghost of King Hamlet (the old king) appearing on the battlements of the castle. He reveals to his son, Prince Hamlet, that he was murdered by his own brother, Claudius, who has since taken the throne and married Hamlet's mother, Gertrude. The ghost demands that Hamlet avenge his death.

Prince Hamlet is deeply troubled by this revelation. He's grieving his father's death and is disgusted by his mother's hasty remarriage. Overwhelmed by the ghost's command, Hamlet struggles with feelings of doubt and uncertainty. He wonders if he can trust the ghost's story and is concerned about the morality of seeking revenge.

To test Claudius's guilt, Hamlet arranges for the staging of a play that mirrors the murder described by the ghost. During the performance, Claudius reacts with guilt and panic, suggestinging that he is indeed the murderer. However, Hamlet's mission for revenge is complicated by his own inner turmoil and hesitation.

To gather more information and possibly discredit Hamlet, Claudius and Polonius, a court advisor, spy on Hamlet. Polonius's daughter, Ophelia, who is also Hamlet's love interest, becomes a pawn in their schemes. Hamlet's erratic behavior is interpreted as madness by those around him, though it's unclear if he's truly insane or just putting on an act.

The play takes a dark turn when Hamlet accidentally kills Polonius thinking he is Claudius spying behind a tapestry. This mistake leads to Ophelia's mental breakdown and eventual suicide. Her brother, Laertes, returns from France and seeks revenge for his father's death, leading to a deadly duel with Hamlet.

The climax of the play comes during the fencing match between Hamlet and Laertes. Unbeknownst to Hamlet, Laertes has poisoned the tip of his sword, and Claudius has also prepared a poisoned drink for him. During the duel, both Hamlet and Laertes are wounded by the poisoned blade. Queen Gertrude accidentally drinks the poisoned wine and dies.

In the final moments, Hamlet confronts Claudius, forcing him to drink the poisoned wine and stabbing him with the poisoned sword. With everyone around him dying, Hamlet succumbs to his own wounds. In his last breath, Hamlet declares Fortinbras, a Norwegian prince, as the next king of Denmark, bringing the play to a tragic close.

Themes and Characters

1. **Hamlet:** The protagonist of the play, Hamlet is known for his philosophical reflections and his famous soliloquy "To be, or not to be". He is a complex character, torn between his duty to avenge his father's death and his own uncertainties about life and death.

2. **Claudius:** The antagonist and Hamlet's uncle, Claudius is the new King of Denmark who has a dark secret. He is ambitious and manipulative, and his guilt over the murder drives much of the play's conflict.

3. **Gertrude:** Hamlet's mother and Claudius's new wife. Her relationship with Hamlet is strained, and her role in the play reflects themes of betrayal and familial loyalty.

4. **Ophelia:** A young woman who loves Hamlet, Ophelia's tragic fate adds to the play's themes of madness and loss. Her relationship with Hamlet and her eventual breakdown are central to the play's emotional impact.

5. **Polonius:** Ophelia's father and Claudius's advisor. He is a meddlesome and somewhat foolish character whose death is a turning point in the play.

6. **Laertes**: Ophelia's brother, who seeks to avenge his father Polonius's death. His quest for revenge parallels Hamlet's and adds to the play's theme of retribution.

7. **Horatio**: Hamlet's loyal friend who provides a contrast to Hamlet's introspective nature. Horatio survives the play and represents a sense of order amidst the chaos.

The Play's Impact and Legacy

Hamlet premiered at the Globe Theatre in London, where Shakespeare's plays were performed. The play was an instant success and quickly became a staple of English theatre. Shakespeare's use of language, complex characters, and deep philosophical themes set *Hamlet* apart from other plays of the time.

One reason *Hamlet* has remained so influential is its exploration of universal themes. Hamlet's struggles with identity, mortality, and ethical dilemmas are relatable to people across different cultures and eras. The play's famous lines and soliloquies, such as "To be, or not to be," have entered the common cultural lexicon, often quoted and referenced in various contexts.

Modern Adaptations

The enduring nature of *Hamlet* has led to numerous adaptations and reinterpretations over the centuries. Filmmakers, playwrights, and other artists have reimagined the play in different settings and formats. From Kenneth Branagh's film adaptation, which presents the play in its entirety, to modern retellings like the film *The Lion King, Hamlet* has been adapted to fit various tastes and eras.

In contemporary culture, *Hamlet* is often explored through different lenses, such as psychological analysis, feminist critique, and political commentary. The play's themes are examined in various educational settings, and its impact on literature, theatre, and popular culture continues to be profound.

Why Hamlet Still Matters

So, why does *Hamlet* continue to resonate today? The play delves into the complexities of human nature and the challenges of decision-making and morality. Hamlet's internal struggle with his duty to avenge his father's death versus his philosophical doubts about life and death mirrors the struggles many people face in their own lives.

The play's rich language, memorable characters, and deep themes offer a window into the human experience, making it relevant across generations. Whether you're interested in drama, literature, or the exploration of complex emotions and situations, *Hamlet* provides a compelling and thought-provoking experience.

In summary, Shakespeare's *Hamlet* is more than just a play; it's a profound exploration of the human condition that has captivated audiences for centuries. Its story, themes, and characters continue to inspire and challenge us, making it a timeless masterpiece in the world of literature.

Playing Style

This version of Hamlet, although reduced to around a one-hour and fifteen minutes playing time, remains true to the original's plot, characters (with some small exceptions), and structure. When performed, this production should maintain a lively pace and exaggerated style.

Technically, the production, as with the original, has a very low level of technical requirements. The sets can be very minimal and the costumes simple. A musical score may be used between scenes to cover changes where necessary.

Of course, one of the major differences between this version and the original is the simplification of the text. On some occasions, in performance, you will find the rhyming scheme helpful to the playing, in which case the actors should just 'stand back', enjoy the words and help the audience do the same. On other occasions, the rhyming scheme will seem stifling and restrictive, in which case do not be afraid to improvise a little, add your own occasional lines or do not emphasise the rhymes so much.

Overall, this version should be fun to play and watch. It can be produced with a small budget and should be done 'over the top' which can give you a chance to play with your own ideas of theatricality.

Cast of Characters

KING CLAUDIUS:	*King of Denmark*
QUEEN GERTRUDE:	*Queen of Denmark, mother of Hamlet*
GHOST:	*of Hamlet's Father*
HAMLET:	*son to the late King, and nephew to Claudius, the present King*
OPHELIA:	*daughter of Polonius*
HORATIO:	*friend of Hamlet*
POLONIUS:	*Lord Chamberlain, advisor to Claudis*
LAERTES:	*son of Polonius*
VOLTIMAND:	*courtier*
CORNELIUS:	*courtier*
ROSENCRANTZ:	*courtier*
GUILDENSTERN:	*courtier*
OSRIC:	*courtier*
A Gentleman:	*cortier*
A Priest	
MARCELLUS:	*an officer*
BERNARDO:	*an officer*
FRANCISCO:	*a soldier*
REYNALDO:	*servant to Polonius*
FORTINBRAS:	*Prince of Norway*
Players:	

- First Player
- King Gonzago
- Queen
- Lucianus

Two Clowns, gravediggers
A Norwegian Captain
English Ambassadors
Lords, Ladies, Officers, Soldiers, Sailors, Messengers, Attendants

Act I

SCENE I.

A platform in front of the castle

[FRANCISCO is standing at his post. BERNARDO enters.]

FRANCISCO
Who's there?

BERNARDO
  It's Bernie. Evening Frank!
How was your night?

FRANCISCO
  Pretty rank!
Nothing to report and freezing cold.

BERNARDO
You can go home now.
  [Pause] Go on, do as you're told!

FRANCISCO
Are you on your own?

BERNARDO
　I'm here with Marcellus.
He's coming up now; that's him by the terrace

FRANCISCO
[Looking]
Who is he with? Someone I know?

BERNARDO
Looks like young Horatio!

FRANCISCO
Horatio? Here? At this time of night?
Do you think we're in trouble?

BERNARDO
　No! It's alright.
He comes up here to meditate.
Now sling your hook[1]; it's getting late!

[Exit FRANCISCO]

[Enter HORATIO and MARCELLUS]

HORATIO
. . . I need to see it with my own eyes!

1　Go away, leave me alone

BERNARDO
Horatio! What a nice surprise

MARCELLUS

[Referring to the GHOST]
I told him ... you know ...

HORATIO
You must be mistaken!

MARCELLUS
Two nights in a row!

BERNARDO
I'm still pretty shaken!

HORATIO
I've come up to see, but I doubt it will show.

MARCELLUS
It first showed up two nights ago.
Bernie, you tell him.

BERNARDO
We were sat around here
About this time of night when the ghost did appear.

[Enter GHOST]

MARCELLUS
And would you believe it? It's just come back!

BERNARDO
It's going to give me a heart attack!

MARCELLUS
You see? I told you; it looks like the King!

[Pause]

[Addressing HORATIO] Well, don't just stand there! Say
     something!

HORATIO
[Addressing the GHOST] What are you that appears this
     night
And looks like the king? You gave us a fright!
Speak, you spirit of the dim!

[Pause]

MARCELLUS
[To HORATIO] I think you have offended him.

BERNARDO
Yes, you have, he's fading away.

[Exit GHOST]

MARCELLUS
You believe me now? What did I say?

HORATIO
Such a cruel and hideous sight.
Something in Denmark's not quite right!

BERNARDO
It's funny you should mention that,
Cos me and the lads were having a chat.
They're recruiting soldiers on the double.
Should we be expecting trouble?

HORATIO
The rumour is that Fortinbras ...

MARCELLUS
The Norwegian king?

BERNARDO
    He is very low class!
We knocked him off and took his pad.

HORATIO
And now his son is really mad.
Young Fortinbras wants everything back.
We think he's planning an attack!
And Denmark's really past its prime.

BERNARDO
So that's why we're on overtime!

HORATIO
We've started getting similar omens
That finished off the mighty Romans:
Apocalyptic horsemen
Warning us of Norsemen.

[Pause]

MARCELLUS
Maybe the ghost came to the fort
To offer us some moral support?

HORATIO
If he was the King, that would make sense.

[The GHOST returns]

MARCELLUS
It's back again: Look! By the fence.

HORATIO

[Addressing GHOST]

If you know something of our fate,
Please tell us now before it's too late!

[The cock crows and GHOST moves to the other side of the stage.]

It's gone again.

BERNARDO
    It's over here!

MARCELLUS
Shall I hit it with my spear?

HORATIO
Only if it will not stand.

[The GHOST moves again.]

BERNARDO
This is getting out of hand!

HORATIO
Here it is!

MARCELLUS

[Trying unsuccessfully to hit the GHOST]

I missed!

[Exit GHOST]

BERNARDO
    It's gone!
Oh, what a bloody carry on!

HORATIO
I think the spear was a mistake.
He was the King, for goodness sake!

MARCELLUS
He was going to speak when the cock did crow.

BERNARDO
They scare ghosts off, didn't you know?

HORATIO
I'm a bit ashamed of what we've done.
Let's go down and find his son.
All things being equal, he should hear about this.

MARCELLUS
Follow me, lads, I know where he is!

[Exeunt]

SCENE II.

The throne room in the castle

[Enter KING CLAUDIUS, QUEEN GERTRUDE, HAMLET, POLONIUS, LAERTES, VOLTIMAND, CORNELIUS]

KING CLAUDIUS
Although the death of my brother is raw,
I've gone and married my sister-in-law.
His demise was a shock, I have to admit,
But it's high time we got over it.
And now I am the ruling class
It's time to deal with Fortinbras.
His Uncle's now king; he's old and he's barmy.
But still, he's in charge of the Norwegian army.
I've written to ask him if he can
Restrain his nephew's battle plan.
Voltimand, Cornelius,
I want you two to deal with this.

[He hands them a letter.]

CORNELIUS AND VOLTIMAND
We'll take this straight to Oslo town.

KING CLAUDIUS
Make sure you do. Don't let me down!

[*Exeunt VOLTIMAND and CORNELIUS*]

What's next upon my list, perchance?

LAERTES
I'd like to travel back to France.

KING CLAUDIUS
Laertes, lad! Have you asked your old man?

POLONIUS
He has that, sire, and I said that he can.
He came back for your coronation,
But now he's lacking stimulation.
It's best if we just let him go.

KING CLAUDIUS
My loyal friend, I won't say no.
And so to Hamlet, who's now my son
And my nephew all in one!

HAMLET
[*Aside*] More than kin and less than kind!

KING CLAUDIUS
Have you got something on your mind?

HAMLET
You could say that.

QUEEN GERTRUDE
[To HAMLET] You miserable git!
It's been two months, get over it!
Stop wearing black and get on board.
You can start by being nice to Claud!
Life always seems a big deal for you!

HAMLET
It 'seems' it, Mum, because it's true!
The clothes I wear they may be dark,
But the pain I feel is far more stark.

KING CLAUDIUS
I understand you feel alone,
But it's time to 'man up', you're still heir to the throne.
Now I'm your dad, so stop your mourning.
Consider this your final warning!

QUEEN GERTRUDE
And forget your University.
You're staying here; we're family!

HAMLET
Whatever you say, I'll try it, Mum.

KING CLAUDIUS
Well, that's all our court business done.
[to HAMLET] You've dropped some of your attitude
And put your mother in a better mood.
We're off for a drink.

GERTRUDE
   [To HAMLET] Goodnight, dear, thanks!

   [Exeunt all but HAMLET]

HAMLET
I'm full of existential angst.
My father died so suddenly,
And took away a piece of me.
Within a month, my mother wed.
His brother Claud now shares her bed.
Daddy Hamlet was a wonderful King,
But they've forgotten everything.
Am I the only one to mourn?
I wish that I had never been born!

   [Enter HORATIO, MARCELLUS, and BERNARDO]

HORATIO
Hail the Prince!

HAMLET
   Horatio?
I thought that you had plans to go
To Wittenberg.

HORATIO
   That's where I was heading.
I came to the funeral and stayed for the wedding.
I was on my way out.

HAMLET

> And what stopped you from leaving?

HORATIO

> *[Hesitant]* I came here to say *[apologetic]* and I know that
>> you're grieving
>
> For your mighty dad!

HAMLET

>   A man amongst men;
>
> We will never see his like again!

HORATIO

> That I saw him last night!

HAMLET

>   Saw who?

HORATIO

>   The old king!

HAMLET

> I think you must be imagining!

MARCELLUS

> He wasn't alive

BERNADO

>   but wasn't quite dead.

HORATIO

> These fellows got me out of bed.

HAMLET
Marcellus, Bernardo, what is this show?

BERNARDO
We saw this strange figure two nights in a row.

HORATIO
They woke me up on night number three
And said that I should go and see
Up on the castles' pinnacle.

MARCELLUS
At first, he was quite cynical!

HORATIO
But sure enough, the ghost appeared
With your father's eyes, his nose, his beard.

HAMLET
And what did he wear?

HORATIO
    His battle gear.

HAMLET
You sure it was him?

HORATIO
    It was really quite clear!

HAMLET
Did he speak?

HORATIO
He had a go
But flew off when the cock did crow.

HAMLET
That is just extraordinary.

MARCELLUS
And that is why we are here. You see?

HORATIO
We thought you'd like to know.

HAMLET
You're right!
Are you on watch again tonight?

MARCELLUS AND BERNARDO
We are, my lord.

HAMLET
I'll join you then.
In case he comes to walk again.

BERNARDO
You'll speak to it?

HAMLET
I'll do my best,
Now keep this quiet and get some rest.

ALL
We will, my lord!

HAMLET

Farewell, Goodnight,
I'll come and see you around midnight.

[Exeunt all but HAMLET]

My father's ghost is on the prowl?
I get the sense of something foul.
Hours, minutes, seconds fly,
Darkness comes and fills the sky.
But no matter how they are concealed,
Evil deeds will be revealed.

[Exit]

CENE III.

A room in Polonius' house

[Enter LAERTES and OPHELIA]

LAERTES
It's time to join my ship at sea.
Ophelia, sister, write to me!

OPHELIA
My letters will greet you back in France.

LAERTES
A word about your new romance
With Hamlet. Things are moving fast,
But a boy's attentions do not last.

OPHELIA
His will I know he fancies me!

LAERTES
But that is not enough, you see.
Even if his heart is loyal,
Do not forget that he still is royal.
He is a slave to obligation,
So look after your reputation.
His attention may be genuine,
But be careful what you give to him!

OPHELIA
As always, your advice is great,
And take it yourself. Temptations await!

LAERTES
I won't be sanctimonious.

OPHELIA
And here is dad!

LAERTES
    Polonius!

                    [Enter POLONIUS]

POLONIUS
Look lively, son; They're ready to sail!

LAERTES
No doubt you've wisdom to avail?

POLONIUS
As always, my son, just a little advice:
Choose your friends wisely or pay the price.
Keep your thoughts close to your chest.
Always look good but not over-dressed.
Neither borrower nor lender be.
And please do not act hastily.
Hold your best friends close to you
And always to yourself be true.
Be a good listener; don't be verbose.
Be friendly to all but don't get too close.
Don't argue too much, but if you do,
Stop others getting the better of you.

Remember these things and you'll be a good man.
Now get on board while you still can!

LAERTES
Goodbye, my lord and my sister. Adieu
[To OPHELIA]
Remember what I said to you!

OPHELIA
It's all in here. *[points to her head]* Don't worry about me.

LAERTES
Right then, it's time to hit the sea!

[Exit]

POLONIUS
So what was your brother talking about?

OPHELIA
Prince Hamlet, of course. That I should watch out

POLONIUS
People in court are asking me whether
You've been spending too much time together.

OPHELIA
He shows me some affection.

POLONIUS
And you show no objection?

OPHELIA
Why should I choose to disbelieve?
He's very sweet.

POLONIUS
You're so naïve!

OPHELIA
He speaks in such an honourable fashion.

POLONIUS
That's just to cover up his passion!

OPHELIA
He swears by heaven he is true!

POLONIUS
That's just to have his way with you!
Let me give you some advice.

OPHELIA
[Sarcastically] Your specialty, it's always nice!

POLONIUS
Hamlet's focus is this nation.
Yours should be your reputation.
He cannot speak with honesty,
So practice much more modesty.
Protect yourself. Do what I say!

OPHELIA
As always, Dad, I will obey!

[Exeunt]

SCENE IV.

The platform in front of the castle

[Enter HAMLET, HORATIO, and MARCELLUS]

HAMLET
The air it bites; it's bitter cold.

HORATIO
It's always nippy here, I'm told.

HAMLET
The time has come, I heard the clock.

HORATIO
Prepare yourself for a bit of a shock!

[Sounds of a party from within]

That's not the ghost; what is that noise?

HAMLET
The king is drinking with the boys.
He's been at it since he left the hall
And I think his band is drunk n' all!
They fanfare him whenever he drinks wine.

HORATIO
Is that a custom?

HAMLET
It isn't mine.
He embraces drink with vim, the King.

HORATIO
It seems to be a Danish thing.

HAMLET
Drunkenness merely distracts
Others from our glorious acts.
I rarely ever touch a beer.

HORATIO
Look, my lord, the Ghost is here!

[Enter the GHOST]

HAMLET
Good or bad, from heaven or hell?
I must ask you and you must tell.
Hamlet, father, royal Dane
Why do you choose to walk again?
In armour dressed you terrify
All stationed here; just tell me why?

[GHOST beckons HAMLET.]

HORATIO
Look. I think it beckons you.

HAMLET
Then I will go.

MARCELLUS
  I wouldn't do!

HAMLET
My life's not worth a jot to me.
My soul will last eternally.
So really, there is nothing to fear.

HORATIO
But what if he takes you somewhere queer,
From where you shall never be seen again,
Leaving you alone and insane?

HAMLET
It waves to me; I have to leave.

MARCELLUS

  [Tugging at HAMLET's sleeve]

You shall not go.

HAMLET
  Get off my sleeve!

  [Drawing his sword]

My mind's made up. Don't make me stay
Or there'll be more than one ghost here today!

  [Exeunt GHOST and HAMLET]

HORATIO
I think his head needs an inspection.

MARCELLUS
Let's follow him; he needs protection.
Something is rotten in the Danish state.

HORATIO
Okay let's go.

MARCELLUS
Before it's too late!

[Exeunt]

 SCENE V.

Another part of the platform

[Enter GHOST and HAMLET]

HAMLET
Where are we going?

GHOST
    Listen well
Before I return to the bowels of hell

HAMLET
Alas, poor ghost!

GHOST
    Please no pity!
Just listen well. This isn't pretty.
I am your father's ghost, you're right!
Doomed to walk the Earth at night
And during the day in purgatory
Where I see things no soul should see.
If ever you did love your old dad,
Get ready to do something bad.
You must revenge the way I died.

HAMLET
Are you suggesting homicide?

GHOST
Murder most foul did do for me.
Not some snakebite near a tree!
The snake that took your father down
Now wears the holy Danish Crown!

HAMLET
I had a feeling it was he.

GHOST
Incest and adultery!
He seduced your mum with wicked ways
And now the queen with him she lays!
My brother stole my loving wife,
And this is how he stole my life:
When I was sleeping somewhere near,
He poured some poison in my ear.
It had a bad effect on me
Like some horrific leprosy.
And before I could my sins repent,
Your father (and your king) was spent.
These hands of mine cannot revenge,
Which is why, my son, you should avenge
My death. So go and kill the so-and-so,
But let your mother Gertrude go.
Leave her in her shame to stew.
Remember me, good son. Adieu!

[Exit]

HAMLET

All you spirits in heaven and hell,

And those that walk the earth as well,

Give me strength, my body fill,

So I can do father's will.

'Remember you?' I think you'll find

That nothing else will fill my mind.

I'll stop your smiling killer flat.

I'll make a little note of that . . .

[Writing] 'Sometimes an outer smile can hide

Something very dark inside'.

At least that's true in Elsinore.

And now to keep the oath I swore.

My father, in my heart you'll stay.

Claudius I will go and slay.

MARCELLUS AND HORATIO

[From within] My lord, my lord,

MARCELLUS

    Are you alright?

HAMLET

Yes I'm fine!

        [Enter HORATIO and MARCELLUS]

HORATIO

    You gave us a fright!

        [Pause]

MARCELLUS
Well, aren't you going to tell us then?

HAMLET
It came, we spoke, it left again.

HORATIO
Oh come on, my lord. Give us a clue.

MARCELLUS
Of what the spirit said to you!

HAMLET
Can you two a secret keep?

HORATIO AND MARCELLUS
You'll never hear from us a peep!

HAMLET
He said that every villain found
Should not be trusted.

MARCELLUS
     How profound!

HORATIO
That's not exactly breaking news!

HAMLET
Let us three share our adieus.
There's nothing more I want to say.
Now leave me be and let me pray!

HORATIO
Leave you now? But where's the sense?

HAMLET
I'm sorry if I cause offence.

HORATIO
Just tell us more about the vision!

HAMLET
I'll say no more; that's my position.
Apart from . . . that the ghost is real.
But trusted friends I really feel
That what we've seen should stay under wraps,
So from here on out, please shut your traps!

HORATIO
Of course I will.

MARCELLUS
   And so will I.

HAMLET
Now cross your hearts and hope to die!

                    [They cross their hearts]

Now swear again.

MARCELLUS
   Again, my lord?

HAMLET
Do it now upon my sword.

GHOST
[Creepy voice from beneath the ground] Swear . . .

HAMLET
> *[Moving above the voice]* from here above the ghostly fella'

Shouting at us from the cellar.

> *[HORATIO and MARCELLUS join HAMLET]*

Now promise me in all good faith
You'll never speak about the wraith.

GHOST
[Creepy voice from beneath the ground] Swear.

HAMLET
> You hear? From under the floor?

He demands that you both pledge some more.

GHOST
[Creepy voice from beneath the ground] Swear!

HAMLET
> *[Moving to the voice once more]* The ghost moves faster now.

Come over here and give your vow.

HORATIO
This night is filled with great unrest.

> *[HORATIO and MARCELLUS join HAMLET]*

HAMLET

And welcome it, just like a guest!
There's more in heaven and earth, you see
Than dreamt of in philosophy.
Now one more thing to tell you both
To add on to your sacred oath.
In the future, however odd
I do behave, so help me God,
Do not react with rolling eyes.
Just play a role and feign surprise.
And never, ever, anywhere
Do speak of this demand.

GHOST

[Creepy voice from beneath the ground] Now swear!!!

[HORATIO and MARCELLUS place their hands on their hearts and bow.]

HAMLET

Unhappy ghost, you may depart.
And gentlemen with all my heart
I thank you both for everything.
I'll pay you back when I am King.
Now let us all go back to court.
There's so much that I need to sort.
My blood it boils, my soul is stirred,
But remember fellas, mum's the word!

[Exeunt]

Act II

SCENE I.

A room in Polonius' house

[Enter POLONIUS and REYNALDO]

POLONIUS
I'm sending you to Paris, Rey,
To give my Laertes cash.

REYNALDO
    Okay!

POLONIUS
But before you meet him personally
Do one more little thing for me.
Go find yourself a Parisian Dane
And ask them nicely to explain
If my son is living right
Or . . . enjoying the pleasures of the night.

REYNALDO
They may think that's suspicious.

POLONIUS
But French food is delicious.

[REYNALDO looks blank]

Go buy them some with lots of wine

And after just the shortest time

They'll tell you all you need know!

REYNALDO
I like that plan.

POLONIUS
    Now off you go!
Just a second, a word to the wise!
Only believe what you see with your eyes.

REYNALDO
I hope he's only playing the flute!

POLONIUS
Well if he is, you can give him this loot!

[Hands over money]

[Exit REYNALDO]

[Enter OPHELIA]

Ophelia dear, are you alright?

OPHELIA
Not really, Dad, I've had a fright.

I was in my room embroidery stitching,
When Hamlet came in all nervous and twitching,
Disheveled and not properly dressed!
He was acting weird and very distressed.

POLONIUS
Please don't say he caused you harm!

OPHELIA
He didn't; he just . . . held my arm
With his outstretched, so plenty of space.
Then he mimed like he was painting my face!
And after that, his head did nod
Three times, I think.

POLONIUS
          That's very odd!

OPHELIA
Then letting out a desperate sigh,
He left and did not say goodbye.

POLONIUS
He's crazed with love it seems, poor lad.
Did you provoke . . .?

OPHELIA
          Of course not, Dad!
I sent his love-notes back unread
To play it cool, just like you said!

POLONIUS

That's what's sent him around the twist.

Oh, why do you do what I insist!

I didn't know his love was true.

I thought he was just playing you.

A word of counsel, Ophelia dear,

For next time your father bends your ear;

Sometimes the older eye it sees

Nothing but conspiracies.

At times the young know more than us!

Come, we'll go tell Claudius.

OPHELIA

You really think he needs to know?

POLONIUS

Don't question me. Come on, let's go!

[Exeunt]

SCENE II.

A room in the castle

*[Enter KING CLAUDIUS, QUEEN GERTRUDE,
ROSENCRANTZ, GUILDENSTERN]*

KING CLAUDIUS
Rosencrantz and Guildenstern!
Undoubtedly you do discern
That Gertrude's son is changed somewhat.
The reasons why we haven't got.
To lose a dad is hard for a son,
But he was my brother, and I'm having fun!
In Hamlet, there is no light, no joy.

QUEEN GERTRUDE
He's just become a miserable boy.

KING CLAUDIUS
You are his friends, that we know.
From many, many years ago.
I suggest a visit to figure out
What his bad mood's all about.
And when you find out, tell us, and then
We can try and cheer him up again.

QUEEN GERTRUDE
And if his temper is resolved,
There'll be a lot of cash involved.

ROSENCRANTZ
Your majesties do not demand,
Which is rare for those in high command.

GUILDENSTERN
Needless to say, we both agree,
And when we succeed, we'll discuss our fee.

KING CLAUDIUS
Let's cure him of his doom and gloom.

QUEEN GERTRUDE
Will someone take them to his room?
It's best if you go instantly.
But you're in for a shock, take it from me!

GUILDENSTERN
I'm sure we've seen him in worse a state.

ROSENCRANTZ
I'm ready to start.

GUILDENSTERN
    And I can't wait.

KING CLAUDIUS
Go make him feel all happy again.

QUEEN GERTRUDE
Yes, cheer him up.

ROSENCRANTZ AND GUILDENSTERN
  We will.

QUEEN GERTRUDE
  Amen!

[Exeunt ROSENCRANTZ, GUILDENSTERN,
and some Attendants]

[Enter POLONIUS]

POLONIUS
The ambassadors have arrived in court
And bring with them their Norwegian report.
In other news, I think I've found
Why Hamlet's sad; it's quite profound!

QUEEN GERTRUDE
It don't think it's a mystery.
[to KING CLAUDIUS] His father died and you married
    me!

KING CLAUDIUS
[to QUEEN GERTRUDE] That view could be quite
    hazardous!

POLONIUS
Let's hear from the ambassadors;
I'll share my news when they have gone.

KING CLAUDIUS
Well show them in, let's get this done!

[Exit POLONIUS]

[Re-enter POLONIUS, with VOLTIMAND and CORNELIUS]

QUEEN GERTRUDE
Welcome, friends,

CORNELIUS
   We're back, my lords.

KING CLAUDIUS
What news from up amongst the fjords?

VOLTIMAND
The Norwegian King is around the bend,
But remains your loyal and trusted friend.
His nephew lied about his goals.
He said he planned to attack the Poles!

CORNELIUS
On hearing the lie, the King was sick,
And had young Fortinbras thrown into the nick[2].
And from his cell, he said it plain:

VOLTIMAND
'I will never attack the Danes again'

---

2   Slang for jail

KING CLAUDIUS
And was the old King satisfied?

VOLTIMAND
So much so he almost cried.
He gave him cash and men of steel
And told him to go attack Poland for real!
It'll give him the chance to let off some steam
And avenge his dad, so it would seem.

CORNELIUS
But as they'll need to cross our land,
He asks you for a helping hand
To grant them passage without fear.

[Giving KING CLAUDIUS a paper]

VOLTIMAND
All the details are written here.

KING CLAUDIUS
At first glance, this all seems alright.
You boys did well; we'll feast tonight.
With Norway appeased, I'd say I've won.
Now let's get this other business done.

[Exeunt VOLTIMAND and CORNELIUS]

[to POLONIUS] You said you know why Hamlet's blue.

POLONIUS
He's a lovesick fool!

QUEEN GERTRUDE

He's a what?

POLONIUS

It's true!

Queen Gertrude, please, just hear me out!

I know for a fact without a doubt.

And after I've read this note to you,

You'll give up on your doubting too.

[Reads] 'Ophelia, yes you are my mate.

Our souls are joined. I think you're great.'

QUEEN GERTRUDE

Did Hamlet write such . . . poetry?

POLONIUS

I know it's bad but stick with me.

[Reads] 'Doubt the stars are made of fire,

Doubt the truth to be a liar,

Doubt the sun is up above,

But never doubt it's you I love.

Dear Ophelia, I am not a poet.

That is clear; I think we know it.

But I love you loads; you are the best,

And I think you have a lovely chest!

QUEEN GERTRUDE

It's clear enough he's mad for her.

KING CLAUDIUS

And her for him?

POLONIUS
That's a good point, sir!
Here I have a confession to make,
But I did what I did for all our sake.

KING CLAUDIUS
You've always been a man of action!

POLONIUS
She told me of their joint attraction
Some days before. I said that he
Was far too lofty for the likes of she.
I mentioned she should take no chances
And spurn the poor boy's amorous advances.

KING CLAUDIUS
Her rejections have driven him around the bend!

QUEEN GERTRUDE
You may be right.

KING CLAUDIUS
But it's not the end!
We have to prove what you say is true.

POLONIUS
I've thought of that; here's what we'll do.
Every day your son hangs out
For hours in the hall without.
I'll send Ophelia there one day
And we'll go too but hide away.
You'll see the power of her love and charm.

And if you don't, I'll go work on a farm.

KING CLAUDIUS
We'll give it a try.

QUEEN GERTRUDE
He's coming, look.
A tragic figure, reading his book.

KING CLAUDIUS
He always looks so bloody grim!

POLONIUS
Please leave. I'll try and speak to him.

[Exeunt KING CLAUDIUS, QUEEN GERTRUDE]

[Enter HAMLET, reading]

Hamlet lad, I have one wish:
For us to speak.

HAMLET
You're selling fish.
Fishmongers are the honest few.
You have a daughter?

POLONIUS
[With confusion] Yes I do!

HAMLET
Look out if she does start to breed.

POLONIUS
[Aside] He's lost the plot. What's that you read?

HAMLET
Words.

POLONIUS
That's nice! And what do they say?

HAMLET
They speak of old men going grey,
Of gaining wrinkles, losing wit.
They lie, but I believe in it.
One day you'll be as old as me
Just like a crab that's from the sea.

POLONIUS
[Aside] More talk of fish. It now seems clear.
He may be mad, but there's method here.
Shall we walk out of the air?

HAMLET
Towards my grave? I'll take you there.

POLONIUS
[Aside]
His madness has a level of sense.
Is he mad for love? He's very intense!
His brain is somehow steelier.
I'll go and get Ophelia.

[To HAMLET]

My lord, I will now take my leave.

HAMLET
Why not my life? I would not grieve.

POLONIUS
Oh look. Your friends!

[Enter ROSENCRANTZ and GUILDENSTERN]

Good timing, chaps.
I think he's had a mental collapse.

[Exit POLONIUS]

ROSENCRANTZ
My honoured lord!

HAMLET
My Rosencrantz
And Guildenstern! What happy chance!
How are you both?

ROSENCRANTZ
We're doing well.

HAMLET
What brings you to this prison cell?

GUILDENSTERN
Prison, my lord? That's hardly fitting.

HAMLET
Denmark's a jail from where I'm sitting.

GUILDENSTERN
All is in close vicinity.

HAMLET
A nutshell is infinity!
You see? It's all just relative!

ROSENCRANTZ
I think it's a lovely place to live.

HAMLET
Why did you come to Elsinore?

ROSENCRANTZ
To visit you.

GUILDENSTERN
    [Guiltily] Yes, nothing more!

HAMLET
For what it's worth, I am delighted.
But you are sure you weren't invited?

GUILDENSTERN
I don't know what to say, your Grace.

HAMLET
No need to speak; I can read your face.
The King and Queen asked you to spy.

GUILDENSTERN
On you?

[Pause]

ROSENCRANTZ

They did!

HAMLET

And I'll tell you why.

I have of late lost all my mirth.

All seems so dark upon the earth.

You see above a sky of blue.

To me it has a darker hue.

We can unsee the brightest star.

Oh, what a piece of work we are!

In a garden of Eden we do reside,

But we only see its darkest side.

[ROSENCRANTZ and GUILDENSTERN giggle]

Did I say something witty?

ROSENCRANTZ

Some players have come here from the city.

The Copenhagen troupe are here,

The ones that humoured you last year.

HAMLET

It's true at times they were quite funny.

But why come here? They're losing money!

GUILDENSTERN

We asked them that only to find

That a younger troupe, once much maligned,

Are now in vogue in the capital city

And taking their money.

HAMLET

Well that's a pity.

My uncle was maligned and all alone

Until he took the royal throne.

Says something about the human whim,

They now all throw their attention at him!

[A fanfare of trumpets from offstage]

GUILDENSTERN

The players are here; they're at the door.

HAMLET

I welcome you both to Elsinore,

My auntie-mum and uncle-dad

Both think that I am raving mad,

But actually it's a part-time thing.

One day I'll tell you everything.

[Enter POLONIUS]

POLONIUS

I have some news to make you happy!

HAMLET

Did you know this man he wears a nappy?

ROSENCRANTZ

They say old men are infantile.

GUILDENSTERN

The actors are here.

POLONIUS
The best by a mile.

HAMLET
Oh God you're dull, Polonius.

GUILDENSTERN
Hamlet, mate, you're riotous!

HAMLET
[To POLONIUS] Like Jephthah, the ancient king,
You've sacrificed the very thing
You held most dear.

POLONIUS
[Aside] My daughter? Still?
The very thing that makes him ill!
The source of all his mind's disruption.

HAMLET
Here comes a timely interruption.

[Enter four or five Players]

Welcome, actors, one and all.
[To a male Player playing a woman] Your 'lady'-ship has
    grown quite tall.
[To another Player] And on your face what has appeared?
Is that supposed to be a beard?
Let's crack on with a little show.

FIRST PLAYER
Which one, my lord?

HAMLET
It's hard to know.
What about the little ditty
You played last year in the city?
I've forgotten much since those brighter days,
But I'll try my best to paraphrase:
'Pyrrhus, who was a killer of course,
Sat inside the Trojan horse,
Looking out for King Priam.

POLONIUS
He really wanted to murder him!

HAMLET
That's all I recall. Player One?

FIRST PLAYER
King Priam he then finds 'anon.
Alighting the nag, Pyrrhus struck.
He missed with his sword but such was his luck
That the wind from the blade swinging down was enough
To down the old King with just one puff.
His blade struck with a fury from hell
And at that same moment, his city fell.

POLONIUS
Is that it?

FIRST PLAYER
No it's not, my friend.

HAMLET

Then let's cut to the emotional end.

FIRST PLAYER

[Very emotionally] His muffled queen . . .

POLONIUS

Oh, 'muffled', that's good!

FIRST PLAYER

Was tearing up the neighbourhood,

Screaming, running up and down,

With a rag for a robe and a cloth for a crown.

Queen Hecuba's husband was brutally slain,

The cruellest of blows . . .

POLONIUS

[Becoming teary] You can say that again!

FIRST PLAYER

[Very dramatically] The cruellest of blows. Her screams
and her cries

Brought tears to even the Deity's eyes.

POLONIUS

[Weeping] Please no more; it's killing me!

HAMLET

[To Player One] And cut! You'll finish presently.

[To POLONIUS] Take care of these men and regain your
reserve.

POLONIUS
I will give them all of the things they deserve.

HAMLET
They deserve no hospitality,
But give them generosity.
Lead them off.

POLONIUS
　　Please walk this way.

HAMLET
Tomorrow we will see your play.

[Exit POLONIUS with all the Players apart from Player One]

[To Player One] But let it be my favourite show,
"The Murdering of Duke Gonzago"

FIRST PLAYER
Of course, my lord.

HAMLET
　　And one more thing,
Could you pop this monologue in?

　　　　　[Gives Player One a script]

It's not too long; just take a look.
You'll have the time to get 'off book'[3]?

FIRST PLAYER
Of course, my lord. I am a pro.

───────────────

3　To memorize the lines so the actors don't have to read the script.

HAMLET

Very well then, off you go.

Polonius' humour may be grim

But please, do not make fun of him.

[Exit Player One]

[To ROSENCRANTZ and GUILDENSTERN] I'll take my
    leave but say once more.

Welcome, both, to Elsinore.

ROSENCRANTZ

Thanks, my lord!

GUILDENSTERN

  We'll leave you be.

HAMLET

You do that, boys; God be with thee.

[Exeunt ROSENCRANTZ and GUILDENSTERN]

This actor's craft brings shame on me.

He summons tears convincingly.

He moves the hearts of all who've seen

With the tale of just some fictional Queen!

Imagine the effect he could've had

If someone had really murdered his dad?

Yet I, with real-life tragedy,

Suffer some strange malady!

Brutally mild and strangely meek,

Not one angry word I speak.

A coward, I know you think I am,

To be upstaged by some old ham.

And you are right! It's time for me
To try to act purposefully.
When watching a play, so I have heard,
Guilty secrets can be stirred
To the point where the audience shout them out.
This is my plan I am talking about!
In tomorrow's performance, I'll ask the lads
To perform a murder like my dad's.
I'll keep my eyes on Uncle Claud.
He'll start to sweat if he's a fraud.
The ghost told me he's guilty,
But that could just be trickery
To damn my soul. The play's the thing!
I will show the truth about this King.

[Exit]

Act III

SCENE I.

A room in the castle

[Enter KING CLAUDIUS, QUEEN GERTRUDE, POLONIUS, OPHELIA, ROSENCRANTZ, and GUILDENSTERN]

KING CLAUDIUS
So tell me, did you figure out
What his madness is all about?

ROSENCRANTZ
He'll only say he is disturbed.

GUILDENSTERN
And when he's quizzed, he gets perturbed.
He starts to act all sly and coy.

QUEEN GERTRUDE
He's always been a petulant boy!
How did he treat you?

ROSENCRANTZ
Like a friend.

GUILDENSTERN
I felt like that was more pretend.

ROSENCRANTZ
I see that, yes, but he wasn't unkind.

QUEEN GERTRUDE
He needs something to amuse his mind.

ROSENCRANTZ
Well, that's a nice coincidence.
A theatre troupe are now with the prince.
We met up with them yesterday
And Hamlet's keen to see their play.

POLONIUS
I agree with him, you really should.
I saw the rehearsal; it was very good.

KING CLAUDIUS
Well if theatre is indeed his 'thing',
We'll watch it too.

ROSENCRANTZ
Very good, my King.

[Exeunt ROSENCRANTZ and GUILDENSTERN]

KING CLAUDIUS
Sweet Gertrude.

POLONIUS

> *[To QUEEN GERTRUDE]* Could you leave, your
> Grace?

KING CLAUDIUS

Our cunning plan we'll put in place.

We've called on Hamlet to appear.

POLONIUS

He'll 'bump into' Ophelia here.

KING CLAUDIUS

Her father and I will hide like spies

Behind the curtain and with our eyes

We'll look to see how he behaves.

POLONIUS

And what brings on his mental raves.

KING CLAUDIUS

Will it be love?

POLONIUS

> I'm sure it will.

QUEEN GERTRUDE

You'll have to both keep very still.

I pray that Ophelia's 'je ne sais quoi'

Is the cause of Hamlet's mental scar.

Don't let this feed your vanity!

OPHELIA

I only want his sanity!

[Exit QUEEN GERTRUDE]

POLONIUS
Right, Ophelia, do as I say.
Walk over there and pretend to pray.
And when Hamlet comes in, act austere
And give your trinkets back, my dear.
[to KING CLAUDIUS] On seeing her love for him has gone
    west
He'll start to freak out. And my case I will rest!
Here he comes; this way, my King.
Let Ophelia take care of everything!

[Exeunt KING CLAUDIUS and POLONIUS]

[Enter HAMLET]

HAMLET
To be or not to be, which one is best?
For stopping our suffering and bringing us rest
From this hell on earth? The choice should be plain.
But what if in death, it all starts again?
And gets worse without end? Now that would just suck!
In a choice of the two, it comes down to luck.
The thought that our fate in death could be worse
Is the only thing keeping us living this curse.
Existing in this place of fear,
Our greatest dreams do disappear
Before they are acted, before they are thought!
But here is Ophelia! A target for sport.

OPHELIA
Hamlet! How are you? Please do tell.
I didn't expect you. Are you feeling well?

HAMLET
Until I saw you, I was feeling quite fine.

OPHELIA
What a fool I was to think you were mine.
My father and brother were right all along.
You never loved me; you were leading me on!
These gifts that you gave me, I now give them back.

[Hands him letters and small gifts.]

Without love they are worthless.

HAMLET
[Sarcastically] Oh alas and alack!
I used to love you.

OPHELIA
Well, that's what you said!

HAMLET
But I lied, you poor thing.

OPHELIA
Then I was misled?

HAMLET
I've naught to take nor give to thee,
So get you to a nunnery,
There to live and not to breed

And spare this world from further greed
And sins found in each chromosome.
Now, where's your dad?

OPHELIA

    He's still at home!

HAMLET
Well, lock him in and throw the key
To spare us all his foolery.

OPHELIA
O heavens help this horrid man.

HAMLET
And if you marry, if you can,
Choose a fool that you'll spit out,
For I will give him reason to doubt
Your purity and chastity.
A nun will suit you perfectly

OPHELIA
O heavens, please restore his grace!

HAMLET
God has made you fair of face,
Which you use to tempt and then say 'no'.
No wonder I've been feeling low.
Now go away and wear a habit
To stop you breeding like a rabbit!

[Exit HAMLET]

OPHELIA
How sad to see the mighty fall.
He once was great, the belle of the ball.
Brains and brawn, a worthy heir,
Admired by all, with lovely hair!
I have no shame to admit I was smitten.
He was my cat and I was his kitten.
But now he is a lunatic!
To be with him it makes me sick.
It's hard for him, but worse for me!
To have seen what I've seen and now see what I see!

[Re-enter KING CLAUDIUS and POLONIUS]

KING CLAUDIUS
Well, I think that it is safe to say
It's not for love he's mad today.
But whatever malady he has got,
He hasn't completely lost the plot.
I suspect a little plan he's hatched.
So I'd like to get him soon dispatched
To England *[Thinks of a faux reason]* to collect some cash
    for me.
His mind will be cleared by the Brits and the sea!
What do you think?

POLONIUS
    Book him a berth!
But if I could add my two-penny worth?
My theory about love could still be true.
And I have a little suggestion too.

[Joining OPHELIA]

Dear Ophelia, don't cause a fuss.

It'll all work out fine, just leave it to us.

We heard every word.

KING CLAUDIUS

And your suggestion is?

POLONIUS

To have Queen Gertrude give him a quiz.

When asked by his mum he'll feel more secure

And offer the clues that we need for his cure.

If it's alright with you, I will eavesdrop once more.

[To KING CLAUDIUS] And of course, if I'm wrong, you
can send him offshore!

KING CLAUDIUS

Whatever we try, it mustn't be botched.

Madness in great ones must not go unwatch'd.

[Exeunt]

CENE II

A hall in the castle

[Enter HAMLET and Players]

[HAMLET hands the Players a script.]

HAMLET
When you play my speech, please don't shout
Or go on waving your arms about.
When the words become dramatic
Just try to be more static.
Don't make your character risible;
He should be recognizable.
The audience should see themselves in you.
That's the only thing an actor should do!
If your style is circumspect,
It will have a far greater effect.
And one more thing I really despise;
Please do not start to improvise!
Or try to hog the light that's lime.
That really is an acting crime.
Not only does it cause delay,
It hides the message of the play.
Let's lose this histrionic spectre!

FIRST PLAYER
Whatever you say boss; you're the director.

[Exeunt Players]

[Enter POLONIUS, ROSENCRANTZ, and GUILDENSTERN]

HAMLET
Is Claudius coming to watch the play?

POLONIUS
He's with your mum. They're on their way!

HAMLET
Well go and help the cast prepare.

[Exit POLONIUS]

And you boys too, go wait back there.

ROSENCRANTZ AND GUILDENSTERN
We will, my lord.

[Exeunt ROSENCRANTZ and GUILDENSTERN]

[Enter HORATIO]

HAMLET
 Horatio!

HORATIO
Hamlet, dear boy, tell me how does it go?

HAMLET
All the better for seeing you.

HORATIO
You're flattering me.

HAMLET
   I've no reason to.
You're as poor as a mouse, next to nothing you've got.
I admire you because you're content with your lot.
And you're always so calm and you're always so stable.
Now, I need you to watch this show if you're able?
A scene like the death of my dad they will act.
Keep a close eye on Claud; how will he react?
If the ghost was right and he's something concealed,
When watching this play, it could be revealed!

HORATIO
I'll watch like a hawk, then compare notes with you.

HAMLET
And here they come now, so go grab a pew!

*[Danish march music plays. A flourish. Enter KING
CLAUDIUS, QUEEN GERTRUDE, POLONIUS, OPHELIA,
ROSENCRANTZ, GUILDENSTERN, and others.]*

KING CLAUDIUS
And here is our Hamlet. How do you fair?

HAMLET
Excellent sir, eating nothing but air.

KING CLAUDIUS
You make no sense.

QUEEN GERTRUDE
Come sit by me.

HAMLET
[Going to sit next to OPHELIA] I'd rather sit on Ophelia's knee.

POLONIUS
You see, my queen? A romantic connection!

OPHELIA
[To HAMLET] Get away from me with your phony affection.

HAMLET
I will ask you now, but don't give me a slap.

OPHELIA
What is it, my lord?

HAMLET
Let me lie on your lap.

OPHELIA
You are strange.

HAMLET
Who, me?

OPHELIA
You go too far.

HAMLET
That's nothing compared to my mama.

My dad's dead two hours, and she laughs like a rake!

OPHELIA
It's two months, not two hours! Don't lie for God's sake!

HAMLET
You remember my dad after sixty days?

OPHELIA
Oh don't be dramatic; save that for the plays . . .
Now sit and be calm, here comes the mime.

HAMLET
[Calming and sitting] Where we get the first clue of who
    did the crime!

[The mime show begins]

*[Enter a Player as King Gonzago and a Player as his Queen
very lovingly, they embrace each other. She kneels and gestures
to him. He joins her and, laying his head on her neck, falls
asleep. She, seeing him asleep, gently lowers him onto a bed
of flowers and leaves. Shortly afterward, the Player Lucianus
comes in, takes off Gonzago's crown, kisses it, pours poison
in the Player King Gonzago's ears, and exits. The Player
Queen returns, finds the Player Gonzago dead, and reacts
with great passion. The Player Lucianus comes in again and
pretends to sympathize with her. The dead body of Gonzago
is carried away. The Player Lucianus woos the Player
Queen with gifts. At first, she spurns his advances, but in the
end accepts his love]*

*KING CLAUDIUS is looking increasingly disturbed.
The Players exeunt.]*

OPHELIA
What does this mean?

HAMLET
    Isn't this fun?
Did we just see a smoking gun?
Here he speaks . . .

[Enter Player One for the prologue]

OPHELIA
    Will we now find out
What that mime was all about?
I've had no time for any reflection.

PLAYER ONE
A tragedy!

[Exit]

OPHELIA
    That was brief!

HAMLET
    Like a woman's affection.

[Enter Player King and Player Queen]

PLAYER KING
Its thirty years since we've been wed,
And very soon I will be dead.
And when I am, find someone new.

PLAYER QUEEN
That's not a pleasant thing to do!
A second husband only quenches the thirst
Of the guilty widow the first!

> *[KING CLAUDIUS is looking increasingly disturbed.]*

HAMLET
[Aside] That's a bit harsh.

PLAYER QUEEN
    And they kill them again
Each time that they kiss their newly found men.

PLAYER KING
You think that now while I'm still clinging on,
But I know that you won't as soon as I'm gone!
Grief and loss distort our brain.
Trust me, love, you'll marry again!

PLAYER QUEEN
I will starve, never rest, and live in despair
Before I remarry. And that, dear, I swear!

HAMLET
She'd better keep that promise now.

PLAYER KING
You've made to me a solemn vow
And now I can sleep in peace with grace.

> *[Sleeps]*

PLAYER QUEEN
No one will ever take your place!

[Exit]

HAMLET
How do you like the play, Mama?

QUEEN GERTRUDE
Her protests go a bit too far.

HAMLET
Now will she go and keep her vow?

KING CLAUDIUS
This play is offensive! We should stop it now!

HAMLET
No, no, it's all light-hearted and fun,
Like me, Papa, your dear stepson.

KING CLAUDIUS
[Looking increasingly agitated] And the play's called . . . .?

HAMLET
            The Mousetrap. You want to know more?
It's basically a metaphor.
A tangled lowly Viennese waltz,
A three-step with royalty, murder, and schmaltz.
Gonzago a duke and Baptista's his wife.
And 'spoiler alert', someone loses their life!
There's no way that that could cause offence
Unless, for some reason, somebody is tense?

[Enter Player Lucianus into the play]

Here's Lucianus, nephew to the king.

OPHELIA
You seem to know most everything!

HAMLET
A few things I know you wouldn't believe.
[to OPHELIA] I've got a few tricks I could put up your
　　sleeve.

OPHELIA
You are naughty, my lord,

HAMLET
　　I'll be punished for that?

OPHELIA
Your jokes, they ascend, but your manners fall flat.

HAMLET
Is that not the ideal mix in a gent?
Let the murders begin!

OPHELIA
　　The actors they went!

HAMLET
But here they come back, they return to avenge.
Let the murdering start. We long for revenge.

[KING CLAUDIUS is looking even more disturbed.]

PLAYER LUCIANUS
All is dark, nobody hears.
Here lies the Duke, I'll poison his ears.

[Pours the poison into the sleeper's ears. KING CLAUDIUS
begins hyperventilating.]

HAMLET
He murders him to get his estate.
The dead one's Gonzago, assigned to his fate.
In later scenes is the suggestion of sex
Between Gonzago's killer and Gonzago's ex.

[KING CLAUDIUS stands, very disturbed and
heads for the door.]

OPHELIA
Claudius stands.

HAMLET
    He's leaving, its certain.

QUEEN GERTRUDE
The king is not well!

POLONIUS
    Let's lower the curtain.

KING CLAUDIUS
Put on the houselights and open the doors!

[Exeunt all but HAMLET and HORATIO.
KING CLAUDIUS howls.]

HAMLET

Something sounds wrong in his terrible roars.

It seems as though the ghost was right.

HORATIO

That is what *I* saw tonight.

HAMLET

Did you watch him during the poisoning scene?

Guilty as hell!

HORATIO

    I know what you mean!

HAMLET

Come musicians, strike up a chord.

Let's sing a ditty to the Lord.

'If the king likes not our little sketch,

We like not him, the miserable wretch'.

[Re-enter ROSENCRANTZ and GUILDENSTERN]

GUILDENSTERN

Hello, my lord. A word with you?

HAMLET

Why only one? Please take a few!

GUILDENSTERN

The king, good sir,

HAMLET

    Oh please, do tell

GUILDENSTERN
He really isn't feeling well.

HAMLET
Then get a doctor to see the cur.
I'd only make him angrier!

GUILDENSTERN
Your mother, you've upset her too.
I think that's why she asks for you.

HAMLET
[Playfully, sarcastically] How nice you are!

GUILDENSTERN
        Please concentrate!
Your mum, she calls.

HAMLET
        I'll make her wait.

ROSENCRANTZ
She said your acts impress her of late.

HAMLET
Did she perhaps extrapolate?

ROSENCRANTZ
She'd like to do that face to face.

HAMLET
I shall obey. I'll go to her place.

ROSENCRANTZ
I'm getting a rather cold vibe from you.

HAMLET
Oh really?

ROSENCRANTZ
    Yes, and that won't do.
I'm just here to find out the cause of your pain
And help to get you right again.

HAMLET
I've nothing much to 'get right' for.

ROSENCRANTZ
You've got the Danish throne in store!

HAMLET
That may be my future, but today that won't do.

*[Re-enter Players with recorders. HAMLET
takes one from them.]*

A recorder, I play one. Guildenstern, you?

GUILDENSTERN
Oh no, my lord.

HAMLET
    Come give it a go.

GUILDENSTERN
Believe me, I can't.

HAMLET

Just take it and blow!

GUILDENSTERN

I know not how.

HAMLET

'Tis as easy as lying.

Just cover these holes, and then toot.

[GUILDENSTERN tries but fails to play the pipe]

You're not trying!

GUILDENSTERN

I know I cannot play this pipe!

HAMLET

Perhaps the Prince is more your type?

You think that you do play him well?

If you did, to you I'd tell

Everything you'd like to know,

You poor deluded so-and-so!

Just like with this little musical tool

You cannot play me . . . for a fool!

[Enter POLONIUS]

God bless you, sir!

POLONIUS

My lord, the Queen!

HAMLET

[Pointing] A camel-shaped cloud you surely have seen?

POLONIUS
[Patronisingly] Yes I have. Quite amazing!

HAMLET
    And now its a weasel.

POLONIUS
Like it's drawn by an artist with paintbrush and easel!

HAMLET
And now like a whale.

POLONIUS
    Like a big Moby Dick!

HAMLET
I'll go see my mother.

POLONIUS
    Yes please, sir, be quick!

HAMLET
In my own time, now go on, you three.

[Exit POLONIUS]

Get out of my hair.

[Exeunt all but HAMLET]

    [Aside] They're toying with me.
It is this time of night that the witches awake,
When the graveyards are lively, when hell starts to shake.
I feel inspired to drink hot blood,
And do evil things. I know that I could.

This may portend the things to come
But now I have to speak to mum!
I hope to show some cruelty
But keep some self-control about me.

[Exit]

SCENE III.

A room in the castle

*[Enter KING CLAUDIUS,
ROSENCRANTZ, and GUILDENSTERN]*

KING CLAUDIUS
His madness, it looks worse to me.
I'm sending him across the sea.

GUILDENSTERN
A great idea!

ROSENCRANTZ
    What else could you do?

GUILDENSTERN
A short sharp shock!

KING CLAUDIUS
    And you're both going too!

GUILDENSTERN
[With surprise] We are?

ROSENCRANTZ
    Are you sure?

KING CLAUDIUS
Are you up to the task?

ROSENCRANTZ
[Feigning resolve] We're going to England!

GUILDENSTERN
We will take a hot flask!

ROSENCRANTZ
And great care of the prince, of course.
His body.

ROSENCRANTZ
His mind.

GUILDENSTERN
His nerves.

ROSENCRANTZ
And his horse!

KING CLAUDIUS
England will give him a stiff upper lip.

ROSENCRANTZ AND GUILDENSTERN
We'd better get going . . .

KING CLAUDIUS
Yes, have a safe trip!

[Exeunt ROSENCRANTZ and GUILDENSTERN]

[Enter POLONIUS]

POLONIUS

I'm off to Gertrude's room, your Grace.

But don't be pulling your jealous face.

I'm following Hamlet, he's gone for that 'chat' . . .

KING CLAUDIUS

She'll give him a grilling.

POLONIUS

    I do not doubt that!

And I will be there, hidden from view

To hear what he says and then come and tell you.

[Exit POLONIUS]

KING CLAUDIUS

Well it's time to come clean, but I know you've all
    guessed.

Yes, I knocked off my brother, but now I can't rest.

I'm like Cain from the Bible but living today!

As guilty as sin and unable to pray!

[He tries unconvincingly to pray.] 'Forgive for my
    fratricide!'?

God doesn't see my gentle side,

Not while I'm living off the spoils

Of my evil murdering toils:

King Hamlet's crown, his castle, his wife.

From the outside it looks like a wonderful life!

But being king is a double-edged sword.

That's why I'll send the prince abroad.

That will get one thing out of my hair.

I'll pray to absolution. *[Looking to heaven]* Please!

Come on legs, bend!

[Kneels and prays]

[Enter HAMLET secretly watching KING CLAUDIUS]

HAMLET
   I could kill him with ease!
My sword through his neck, an effective attack.
But that wouldn't be paying my father back.
To kill him after he'd made his amends
Would mean he and our Lord and the saints are all
     friends.
My father was killed without having a shot
At repenting *his* sins, and he had a lot!
No, I'll wait till he's whoring, or gambling, or worse,
Then kill and condemn him to an eternal curse.
My mother awaits. I will leave him to pray.
I will grant him some time, just a temporary stay!

[Exit]

KING CLAUDIUS
My words fly up, my thoughts remain low.
Words without thoughts never heavenwards go.

[Exit]

SCENE IV.

The Queen's chamber

[Enter QUEEN GERTRUDE and POLONIUS]

POLONIUS
He's coming here now, so take my advice;
Be harsh on the boy. You've tried being nice.

HAMLET
[offstage] Mother, Mother.

QUEEN GERTRUDE
    I'll do what you say.

POLONIUS
And I'll hide over here not to get in the way.

[POLONIUS hides behind a curtain.]

[Enter HAMLET]

HAMLET
Now, what is it, Mum?

QUEEN GERTRUDE
    You've offended your pa!

HAMLET
And you've married his brother. That's much worse, by
    far!

QUEEN GERTRUDE
You know who I mean. It was I gave you life!

HAMLET
My mother, my queen, and my uncle's new wife!

QUEEN GERTRUDE
If you can't speak politely, I will call others in.

HAMLET
[Showing a dagger] Sit down over here and atone for your
    sin.

QUEEN GERTRUDE
Do you plan? No, you wouldn't? You couldn't kill me!
[Screams] Hamlet's on a killing spree!

POLONIUS
[Behind the tapestry] A what? Hang on . . .

HAMLET
    Somebody's there *[Drawing his sword]* in the drapes.
This will put an end to your japes.

        [Makes a stab through the tapestry.]

POLONIUS
[Behind] I am slain!

        [Falls and dies still unseen.]

QUEEN GERTRUDE
    Oh my God, Hamlet, what have you done?

HAMLET
Has the King been killed by his own stepson?

QUEEN GERTRUDE
A bloody deed.

HAMLET
   As bad, or obscene
As killing a king and bedding his Queen?

QUEEN GERTRUDE
As killing a king?

HAMLET
   Yes, that's what I said!

   [Lifts up the tapestry and discovers POLONIUS.]

I've gone and killed Polonius dead!
I thought it was King Claudius, see?
But he had it coming. Now where were we?
So much to share. How shall we start?
When did you get such callous a heart?

QUEEN GERTRUDE
After what you've just done, you're still torturing me?

HAMLET
Your act has destroyed all modesty!
You've turned your virtue inside out.

QUEEN GERTRUDE
I don't know what you are talking about!

HAMLET

[Points to a picture on the wall depicting the following]

Look at this cheap piece of art:
Two brothers are shown but set well apart.
One is heroic, the other a leech.
You recognise both.

QUEEN GERTRUDE
What point do you reach?

HAMLET
You chose the lowly parasite.
What happened? Did you lose your sight?
Your hearing, taste, your smell, and touch?
No other woman has lost so much!
The choice that you did fashion
It wasn't born of passion.
You're far too old for that, my dear.
So tell me, what *did* happen here?
I'll give you one concession,
That it could be dark possession.
If the devil, he can cause this fuss,
What hope then for the rest of us?

QUEEN GERTRUDE
O Hamlet, please don't speak that way;
My sins will never wash away.

HAMLET
They're in your heart, your soul, your head,
Like the stink in your sullied bed.

QUEEN GERTRUDE
My mind it does unfasten!

HAMLET
You married an assassin!
A man not worthy to kiss the feet
Of the one he killed and stole his seat.

QUEEN GERTRUDE
Please say no more. You've cruelly lied.

HAMLET
[Enter GHOST, seen only by HAMLET] And here he is, your
man who died.

QUEEN GERTRUDE
[Aside] I swear to God, he's lost the plot.

GHOST
[To HAMLET] Don't torture her; she's suffered a lot.

HAMLET
I'll focus on the job at hand.

QUEEN GERTRUDE
Hamlet, I don't understand.

GHOST
Your mum is scared; She's had a fright.
So comfort her . . .

HAMLET
      [To QUEEN GERTRUDE] Are you alright?

QUEEN GERTRUDE
Am *I* alright? Look at your hair.
It stands bolt upright. And you talk to the air!

HAMLET
[To QUEEN GERTRUDE] Look at how he glares at me!
[To the GHOST] Please tone down your intensity!

QUEEN GERTRUDE
To whom do you speak?

HAMLET
  To him right there?

QUEEN GERTRUDE
There's nothing at all; it is only thin air.

HAMLET
What do you hear?

QUEEN GERTRUDE
  Just what you say.

HAMLET
Look there he goes now, stealing away!
Like my father, but much, much more,
And now he's going out of the door!

[Exit GHOST]

QUEEN GERTRUDE
Hamlet, you hallucinate.

HAMLET
A lunatic cannot restate
Their words. But I know what I said!
Believe me, I am right in the head.
Claiming I'm a lunatic
Convinces no one you're not sick.
Confess your crime, apologize,
Or God in Heaven will damn your eyes!

QUEEN GERTRUDE
Oh Hamlet, you do break my heart.

HAMLET
Then throw away its worser part
And keep the half that still is good,
The part that I know that never would
Sleep again in my uncle's bed,
No matter that you now are wed.
I beg you, Mum, just try and quit.
Abstain and you'll get used to it

[Pointing to POLONIUS]

I'm sorry about Polonius,
But fate *did* have a hand in this.
This is bad, but there's worse to come

QUEEN GERTRUDE
What shall I do?

HAMLET
    Just listen, Mum;
Stay out of your husband's arms.

Don't let him use his evil charms
To lure my secrets out of you.
That's the only thing that you must do!

QUEEN GERTRUDE
Like a safe without a key,
Your secrets are secure in me.

HAMLET
I'm going to England; did you know of that plot?

QUEEN GERTRUDE
My husband did tell me but then I forgot.

HAMLET
A couple of 'friends' with me I'll take.
I trust them like I trust a snake.
They'll try to make my journey hard
But I'll hoist them on their own petard[4].
I'll be killing two birds with one small stone!
I'll now be leaving you alone.

[Picking up POLONIUS' body]

His advice he keeps to himself at last
And I'll get rid of his body fast.
Come now sir, off to your leisure.
Goodnight, Mama, it is always a pleasure.

[Exit HAMLET dragging POLONIUS]

---

4   Literally this means to blow someone up with a bomb they made. Idiomatically, it means someone sees the negative consequences of their own actions. The phrase was invented by Shakespeare.

Act IV

SCENE I.

A room in the castle

[Enter KING CLAUDIUS, QUEEN GERTRUDE,
ROSENCRANTZ, and GUILDENSTERN]

KING CLAUDIUS
He's just got such a miserable face.
He needs cheering up.

QUEEN GERTRUDE

[To ROSENCRANTZ and GUILDENSTERN]

Please give us some space.

[Exeunt ROSENCRANTZ and GUILDENSTERN]

My lord, what I have seen tonight!

KING CLAUDIUS
Hamlet?

QUEEN GERTRUDE
Yes, what a terrible sight.
He came to my room in a raging fit,
Shouting at me and forced me to sit,
And then something erroneous ...
He went and killed Polonius
Who was hiding behind a tapestry!

KING CLAUDIUS
Bloody hell! That could have been me!
You know they'll blame me for not reining him in.
I just love him too much, is that really a sin?
I let him rant, I let him rave.
And where is he now?

QUEEN GERTRUDE
He's preparing a grave.

KING CLAUDIUS
He's disposing of the body, of course!

QUEEN GERTRUDE
I think that shows a little remorse.

KING CLAUDIUS
As soon as the sun does bring in the day,
He will be on that ship, and we'll wave him away.
It will take some explaining, this murderous turn.

[Re-enter ROSENCRANTZ and GUILDENSTERN]

But we don't have much choice. You're back,
Guildenstern!

GUILDENSTERN
With Rosencrantz.

KING CLAUDIUS
    Do this for me:
Go down to the cemetery.
Hamlet is there preparing a tomb
For Polonius, who today he killed in her room.

QUEEN GERTRUDE
Take the body from my eye's little apple,
And bring it back here to lay in the chapel.

[Exeunt ROSENCRANTZ and GUILDENSTERN]

Come, let's share with the great and the good,
What's happened in our neighbourhood.
And tell them our plan for after today.
My soul is full of discord and dismay.

[Exeunt]

SCENE II.

Another room in the castle

[Enter HAMLET]

HAMLET
The body it is now interred.

ROSENCRANTZ AND GUILDENSTERN:
[Offstage] Hamlet! Can we have a word?

HAMLET
Who calls me there? Oh here they come.
Tweedledee and Tweedledum!

[Enter ROSENCRANTZ and GUILDENSTERN]

ROSENCRANTZ
You should say what you've done with the corpse.

GUILDENSTERN
    Yes, you must!

HAMLET
Ashes to ashes, dust to dust.

ROSENCRANTZ
We need to take it to the shrine.

HAMLET
You think I'll obey your wishes or mine?
If you disagree, be my guest, take a lunge.
I'm unlikely to fall at the hands of a sponge.

ROSENCRANTZ
A sponge, my lord?

HAMLET
    Filled with Kings wishes,
Which he will then squeeze and leave for the dishes.

ROSENCRANTZ
I don't understand.

HAMLET
    That's abundantly clear.
Clever words die in a foolish man's ear!

ROSENCRANTZ
Give us the body, to the king we must bring . . .

HAMLET
The king's not a body; the king is a thing.

GUILDENSTERN
A thing, the king?

HAMLET
    Or a no-thing perhaps?
Either way it's the same, just take me there, chaps!

[Exeunt]

CENE III.

Another room in the castle

[Enter KING CLAUDIUS with some attendants]

KING CLAUDIUS
How dangerous is man when his mind it warps.
They search for him and for the corpse.
He's clearly not right mentally,
But we have to treat him gently.
The public like their precious Prince.
They'll no doubt claim his innocence.
They judge with their hearts and not with their brains.
We'll send him away untied, not in chains.
A diplomatic trip it will seem,
But his final cure . . . will be extreme.

[Enter ROSENCRANTZ]

What's happened?

ROSENCRANTZ
    I'm sorry. We can't find the body.

KING CLAUDIUS
And where is the prince?

ROSENCRANTZ
Outside in the lobby.

[Enter HAMLET and GUILDENSTERN]

KING CLAUDIUS
Where did you leave Polonius?

HAMLET
Don't be acrimonious!
He's at lunch.

KING CLAUDIUS
Where?

HAMLET
Under the ground,
Being eaten by insects and worms, I'll be bound.
You can fish with a worm that has fed on a king,
Then eat fish that has fed on that very same thing.

KING CLAUDIUS
Could you explain that to me, by any chance?

HAMLET
A king may ascend via a poor beggar's pants.

KING CLAUDIUS
Just tell me where's Polonius?

HAMLET
It's all rather harmonious.
He's in heaven, with God, any angel will tell.

But if you don't find him there, you can go straight to hell.
And if he's not there, in just three weeks or four,
Just follow his smell up to your second floor.

KING CLAUDIUS
You two go and find him there.

[To some Attendants]

HAMLET
Don't rush, he's not going anywhere.

[Exeunt Attendants]

KING CLAUDIUS
Your actions with Polonius
Were definitely felonious,
So we've brought forward your leaving date.
Your boat is ready, don't make it wait.

HAMLET
For England!

KING CLAUDIUS
        Yes

HAMLET
        That's good!

KING CLAUDIUS
        It is?
We have the finest purposes.

HAMLET

Your purposes I know what kind.

I have an angel who reads your mind.

Goodbye. Mama, we'll beat the swell.

KING CLAUDIUS

I am your dad.

HAMLET

My mum as well:

Husband and wife, one body, one flesh;

And so you're my mother. I'll go where it's fresh.

[Exit]

KING CLAUDIUS

Get him on that boat today

And make darn sure it sails away.

Everything else is already in place.

Don't stand there gawping; go on, make haste!

[Hands ROSENCRANTZ and GUILDENSTERN a letter.]

[Aside] Now, King of England, I hope it's true

You'll obey the instructions I'm sending to you

Asking you to kill the prince.

You do not want the consequence

Of letting him live. So don't delay;

Make sure he's gone within the day.

He ruins my plans and plagues my brain.

I will get no peace until he is slain.

[Exuent]

CENE IV.

A plain in Denmark

[Enter FORTINBRAS, a Captain, and Soldiers, marching]

PRINCE FORTINBRAS
Right then, Captain, no more fuss.
Go and tell King Claudius.
He needs to make his promise good
And let us in his neighbourhood.
Tell him we can meet face-to-face.
Just to set the time and name the place

CAPTAIN
[With a flourish]
Say no more. I'm on it, squire!

PRINCE FORTINBRAS
Why do these men I bother to hire?

　　　　　[Exeunt FORTINBRAS and Soldiers]

　　　　　[Enter HAMLET, ROSENCRANTZ,
　　　　　　GUILDENSTERN, and others]

HAMLET
Good sir, come here. What is this force?

CAPTAIN
We are the army of the Norse.

HAMLET
So what are you doing in Denmark, man?

CAPTAIN
It's part of our invading-Poland plan.
Your uncle Claud said it was OK
To pass through Denmark on our way.
Young Fortinbras is avenging his dad,
Getting Norway back some land that was grabbed.
It's the only heroic thing to do.
I think his old man would be proud, don't you?

HAMLET
[Aside] Thousands of ducats and innocent souls
Will be lost to this pointless feud with the Poles.
A tooth for a tooth and an eye for an eye,
It's not a good reason for thousands to die!

CAPTAIN
I'd better be off, and thanks for the chat.
[Aside] I told him too much; I always do that!

[Exit]

ROSENCRANTZ
We'd better go too. No time to delay.

HAMLET
I'll catch you both up; we've still got all day.

[Exeunt all except HAMLET]

All I see are signs from fate
Suggesting that I should not wait
To get revenge! But what is man
If he does not carry out a plan?
I'm motivated, full of wit,
And I'm surely over-thinking it!
These Norse have no good reason to kill
And yet they find some iron will.
It's not just down to intellect.
Sometimes your honour you have to protect.
Shame on me, my father was slain,
My mother defiled, and I only complain.
From now on I'll act and cast doubt aside.
My hesitant thoughts I will just override!

[Exit]

 SCENE V.

A room in the castle

[Enter QUEEN GERTRUDE, HORATIO, and a Gentleman]

QUEEN GERTRUDE
I really can't do this today.

GENTLEMAN
I am sorry, Ma'am. She won't go away.
She trembles and shakes, with a moan and a shout!

QUEEN GERTRUDE
And what's she going on about?

GENTLEMAN
We think she speaks about her dad
But it's hard to tell . . . she's stark raving mad!
She beats her own body, gestures wildly and winks.

HORATIO
It's probably better to see her, methinks.

QUEEN GERTRUDE
Then let her come in.

[Exit HORATIO]

[Aside] to torture me more!

How many more trials do these days have in store?

[To herself] Just continue to act as though nothing is wrong

But its harder to do, the more this goes on!

[Re-enter HORATIO, with OPHELIA who looks very troubled]

OPHELIA
Where is the Queen with the haunting eyes?

QUEEN GERTRUDE
Ophelia, what a pleasant surprise!

OPHELIA
  [Sings] How can you tell your love is true?
  By the look of his hat and the style of his shoe!

QUEEN GERTRUDE
And what does that song mean, my dear?

OPHELIA
You'll figure it out; just lend me an ear!
  [Sings] He is dead and gone, deceased and alone
  At his head a green turf, at his heels is a stone.

               [Awkward silence]

Here comes some more . . .

QUEEN GERTRUDE
  Ophelia, no!
  [Sings] His shroud is as white as the high mountain snow,

[Enter KING CLAUDIUS]

QUEEN GERTRUDE
Ophelia's been singing;

HORATIO
It feels like for hours!

OPHELIA
[Sings] Covered with the sweetest flowers
Which did not fall upon the floor.

KING CLAUDIUS
Ophelia! Please don't sing any more.

OPHELIA
The baker's daughter was an owl, you see.
We know who we are but not who we'll be.

KING CLAUDIUS
I think she's speaking about her dad.

OPHELIA
No talk of that; it's very bad!
If you're asked what it means, this you should say:
A song about Saint Valentine's Day,
[Sings] All in the morning
I came without warning
To be his little Valentine.
He let me in; I made him mine.
That very moment my innocence spurned,
He let in a maid, who never returned.

KING CLAUDIUS
Please, Ophelia!

OPHELIA
I'm nearly done.
For the sake of God, I'll carry on,
    [Sings] Alack and fie on men for shame!
    They ruin us and are to blame.
    Before they take us to their bed,
    They promise us that they will wed.
    Then after, they refuse and say
    You would be my wife, if I'd not got my way!

KING CLAUDIUS
Do we have to see this 'song and dance'?

OPHELIA
You need to show some tolerance.
I go mad when I think of the blunder
That's left my dad lying six feet under!
To my brother I will now tell.
I leave, sweet lady; fare thee well.

[Exit]

KING CLAUDIUS
Keep an eye on her.

[Exit HORATIO]

    Why do I bother?
If it's not one thing, then it's another.
Her dad being killed just started the day. *[pointing to
    OPHELIA]*

And then her son got sent away.
He may have got a famous name,
But he's only got himself to blame.
I did make a mistake with Polonius.
His funeral was unceremonious.
Now Ophelia is pretty rough.
And as if all that wasn't bad enough,
Her brother has just got back from France
And he'll kill me given half a chance!
He'll been told that I ran his father through,
But it's the only thing I *didn't* do!
It's not so easy being King.
You get the blame for everything!

[A noise offstage]

QUEEN GERTRUDE
What is that rumpus? Holy cow!

KING CLAUDIUS

[Enter another Gentleman]

Oh bloody hell, what is it now?

GENTLEMAN
Save yourself, Your Majesty!
Laertes' men are chasing me!
He plans to be King; they've started a coup,
And the people want him, they don't like you.
They are yelling and throwing their hats in the air,
And chanting his name like they just don't care!

QUEEN GERTRUDE
Those Danish dogs!

GENTLEMAN
It's looking bad

KING CLAUDIUS
The doors are broken!

[Noise within]

[Enter LAERTES, armed, Danes following]

LAERTES
Where is my dad?

KING CLAUDIUS
I'm afraid he's dead, but we're not to blame!

LAERTES
Then who knocked him off? Just give me a name!
Until he's revenged, I will not be his son!

QUEEN GERTRUDE
Trust us, young man; we will help get this done!

GENTLEMAN
[Within] Let her come in.

LAERTES
How now! Who's this?

[Re-enter OPHELIA]

Oh dry my brains! Is that my sis?!

My revenge will be a double hit,
For my father's life and sister's wit.

OPHELIA

    [Sings] Uncovered to his grave he did go

    Hey nonny, nonny, nonny; no

    And in his grave rained many a tear:

    Farewell, my dove, my dad, my dear!

LAERTES

Every note it stirs my blood
To act like all betrayed sons should!

OPHELIA

    [Sings] You must now sing 'and-down and-down',

    And then call him 'to ground to ground'

    A song to end this ritual slaughter

    Like the steward who stole his boss' daughter

    [To QUEEN GERTRUDE] Here are pansies for
        thought, and rosemary,

And fennel for adultery.

Here are daisies, they will suit you too,

But violets they will dry on you.

They symbolize fidelity.

    [Sings] You'll always be Sweet Robin to me.

LAERTES

Her mind is lost in deep distress,
But even this she does with finesse!

OPHELIA

    [Sings as she exits] And will he e'er not come again?

He now sits on a higher plain.

His breath, his life, my heart he stole.

God have mercy on his soul!

[Exit]

LAERTES

You see this pain? Beyond belief!

KING CLAUDIUS

Trust me, we do share your grief.

Go bring your trusted colleagues hence,

For they shall judge my innocence.

If they think I am guilty, along with my wife,

We'll give up our crowns, this land, and this life.

But if our innocence it is learned,

We will not leave one stone unturned.

LAERTES

His death seems so capricious.

KING CLAUDIUS

You're right to be suspicious.

The guilty ones I swear will pay.

I beg you sir, with me, away.

[Exeunt]

SCENE VI.

Another room in the castle

[Enter HORATIO and a Servant]

HORATIO
A letter from abroad? Who brought it again?

SERVANT
Sailors, sir, big salty men!

HORATIO
Then let them in . . .
[Aside] From outside this land?
They can only be from Hamlet's hand.

[Enter Sailors]

HORATIO
Aye, aye, sailors. What do you know?

FIRST SAILOR
Are you the Lord Horatio?

HORATIO
I am.

FIRST SAILOR
Then I should hand this over.
I got it on our voyage to Dover.
[Knowingly] From important royalty!

HORATIO
Very good, now give it to me.
[Reads] 'Read this letter, then at the end
Get these sailors to the King, my friend.
Ignore all their 'me timbers' and 'shiver'.
I gave them letters to deliver.
Now read these words most carefully.
They will tell you exactly what happened to me.
Just two days into our excursion,
Our ship received a hostile incursion.
Some pirates they did steal me away.
(but don't worry, I've been treated okay!)
They promised to keep me safe on board
If they could get to speak to Claud.
Once they've done that, they will bring you to me.
Those treacherous two are still at sea,
Heading for England. Rosencrantz
And Guildenstern are sailing past France.
Fair winds to you to get this done.
Then you'll hear my tales, which will cast you dumb.
I really cannot wait to tell
So get a move on, fare thee well.
Signed. Hamlet the prince.'
     Come salty crooks.
To see the king, let's sling our hooks!

[Exeunt]

SCENE VII.

Another room in the castle

[Enter KING CLAUDIUS and LAERTES]

KING CLAUDIUS

> *[Finishing his explanation]*

So please with me don't be unruly.

His intended victim was yours truly!

LAERTES

If that is true and has some worth,

Why do you let him walk the earth?

KING CLAUDIUS

Good question and a tricky one,

The first thing is, he's Gertrude's son.

If I killed him, then she'd kill me!

And I can't be having that you see!

The second reason is the people;

They shout his name from every steeple.

Their love for him is vivid.

If I killed him, they'd be livid!

LAERTES

Well, I have lost my noble dad,

And my beautiful sister has now gone mad.

KING CLAUDIUS
I know that, and I loved him too.
I promise that I will work with you,
To bring the callous murderer down.

[Enter a Messenger]

MESSENGER
Letters, my lord, from out of town:
Notes from Hamlet to you and the Queen.

[Receiving letters]

KING CLAUDIUS
From Hamlet! Who brought them?

MESSENGER
    Sailors *[pointing offstage]* unseen:
They gave them to me, and I brought them in here!

KING CLAUDIUS
Laertes can stay, but you disappear!

[Exit Messenger]

[Reads] 'High and mighty, understand:
I am naked back in my land.
Tomorrow we'll meet and you will learn
The story behind my sudden return!
Signed Hamlet'. 'I'm naked?' What should this mean?
You think it is true? Or is it a scheme?

LAERTES
I've no idea, but let him nigh
So I can look him in the eye.

KING CLAUDIUS
I'll let him enter, but do him no harm!

LAERTES
Just don't expect me to be calm.

KING CLAUDIUS
Quite the opposite. I have made it my mission
For Hamlet to die with zero suspicion.
Not even his mother will suspect foul play.

LAERTES
So what is your plan?

KING CLAUDIUS
     I was just going to say!
Word has it that with the sword you are blessed.
Hamlet's always been jealous of your fencing prowess.
He would surely love to spar with you.
We'll set up a contest for tomorrow at two.
He'll enter the bout with his customary swagger
And won't see that we've sharpened only one dagger.
The one he will choose we'll arrange to be blunt,
And with just one stab you'll murder the runt.

LAERTES
And just to be sure that the plan he can't spoil,
I will put some strong poison on the end of the foil.

All it will take is his arm to be scratched
For his murderous soul to be duly dispatched.

KING CLAUDIUS
And you may say this is overkill,
But I have another idea still.
With all that sparring and the heat in the palace,
He'll get hot. Call for water, and I'll give him a chalice.
Which I'll with poison; he will die on the spot!
It's a three-in-one death. Pretty good, is it not?

LAERTES
I'm finally calmed.
> *[Crying from offstage, approaching]* But what is that
> sound?

> *[Enter QUEEN GERTRUDE]*

KING CLAUDIUS
It's Gertrude, the Queen.

QUEEN GERTRUDE
> Your sister has drowned!

KING CLAUDIUS
Oh bloody hell!

QUEEN GERTRUDE
> We are living a curse!

KING CLAUDIUS
My luck it goes from bad to worse!

LAERTES
Where did it happen?

QUEEN GERTRUDE
   In a babbling brook.
I sent some men to take a look.
She'd made a garland called 'dead men's fingers',
Started humming a tune . . .

LAERTES
   She was one of life's singers!

QUEEN GERTRUDE
Then she lay in the water in all of her clothes.

KING CLAUDIUS
Did she know that was dangerous?

QUEEN GERTRUDE
   Nobody knows!
But in no time at all, just away from the bank,
Her clothes filled with water and your sister . . . she sank!
She drowned!

KING CLAUDIUS
   She's dead?

QUEEN GERTRUDE
   She is, poor dear.

LAERTES
She is wet enough. I should not shed a tear.
But I'm human, with feelings, they have to be shed.

But once they are out, some words will be said!

[Exit]

KING CLAUDIUS
Well thanks a lot, Gertrude. Your timing is great.
I know it's important but couldn't it wait?
I'd just calmed him down; it's a right horror show.
Let's see where he went.

QUEEN GERTRUDE
   How was I supposed to know?

[Exeunt]

Act V

SCENE I.

A churchyard

[Enter two Clowns with spades]

FIRST CLOWN
They said 'Christian funeral', but I think they lied
Given that it was suicide!

SECOND CLOWN
The coroner said there was no offence!

FIRST CLOWN
So she drowned herself in self-defence?

SECOND CLOWN
It seems like she either pushed herself in,
Or the water attacked her and she couldn't swim.

FIRST CLOWN
It all sounds very fishy to me.

SECOND CLOWN
Not really. She was royalty!
For them the Lord does bend his rules
In a way he won't for us poor fools.
But back to work. Enough of that.

FIRST CLOWN
Let's dig like Adam, the first aristocrat!

SECOND CLOWN
Aristocrat? He had no arms[5]!

FIRST CLOWN
What did you say? You must be Brahms[6]!
The Scripture says that 'Adam dug'[7]
He couldn't do that with no arms, you mug!

[They laugh.]

SECOND CLOWN
That's pretty good!

FIRST CLOWN
    You want one more?

---

5   Arms as in a coat of arms, which only nobles would have.

6   Cockney rhyming slang for pissed/drunk. Liszt rhymes with pissed and Brahms and Liszt is shortened to Brahms.

7   Genesis 2:15 says Adam tended the garden. The clown is jokingly calling this digging.

SECOND CLOWN
Sure. Why not? A little encore.

FIRST CLOWN
What craftsman's the strongest in all of his acre?

SECOND CLOWN
That's got to be the gallows-maker,
Cos of all the skilled and hefty fellas,
His structures outlive thousands of dwellers.

FIRST CLOWN
The gallows are strongest just for the sinner!
The church is for all,

SECOND CLOWN
    which makes it the winner!
The stonemason's the answer?

FIRST CLOWN
    No, sorry, that's wrong.
Have one more guess.

SECOND CLOWN
    Got it!
[Pause. He tries to recall but cannot.] It's gone!

    [Enter HAMLET and HORATIO, at a distance]

FIRST CLOWN
I'll tell your answer, with no more delay:
Graves house their tenants until judgement day . . .

SECOND CLOWN
So it's us!

FIRST CLOWN
    You're a genius. Now go get us a beer.
I'll take care of things around here.

[Exit Second Clown]

[He digs and sings merrily.]

    In youth, when I loved, I thought we would meet
    I imagined a wedding. That would have been sweet!

HAMLET
[with HORATIO spying] Would you look how this old man
    behaves,
Singing songs while digging graves!

HORATIO
I suppose to him they're just a few holes.

HAMLET
Only toffs[8] can afford to have sensitive souls!

FIRST CLOWN
    [Sings] But age it did catch me, I could not have
        resisted.
    And it buried me deep like I never existed.

[Throws up a skull]

---

8   A rich or upper-class person

HAMLET

Look how he treats these human remains.

They once had flesh with tongues and brains.

Lawyers, politicians, *and* god-fearing souls

Are now no better than bowling balls.

FIRST CLOWN

> *[Sings]* A pickaxe, a spade, and some dirt for a
> shroud.
>
> One skull is enough but two are a crowd.

> *[Picks up another skull, throws one away, and
> jumps in the grave.]*

HAMLET

Those skulls to him are just a prop.

I feel like I should make him stop.

[Appearing and addressing the First Clown] Whose grave is
this, sir?

FIRST CLOWN

What? This one here?

[Pointing at HAMLET] It's for a guest, like you, my dear.

HAMLET

But you're the one who's lying in there.

FIRST CLOWN

I am indeed. Then it's mine, I fear.

HAMLET

But you look like one of the liveliest men.

And graves are for stiffs; so you are *lying* again!

FIRST CLOWN
These lies are racing through the air.

HAMLET
What man is going to rest in there?

FIRST CLOWN
    No man, sir.

HAMLET
Then a woman. Which one?

FIRST CLOWN
No one, sir, her days are done!

HAMLET
These peasants are cheeky; can't say I'm a fan.
How long have you been a grave-digging man?

FIRST CLOWN
I graduated top of my class
The day King Hamlet beat Fortinbras.

HAMLET
And when was that?

FIRST CLOWN
    Every fool knows.
The day young Hamlet first showed his nose.
He's mad now, of course, and was sent overseas
To England.

HAMLET

But why?

FIRST CLOWN

To get sane, if you please!

But if he stays mad, he will fit right in.

They are all barmy in England, so it's a big 'win-win'.

HAMLET

How come he went crazy?

FIRST CLOWN

He just lost his mind.

HAMLET

On what grounds?

FIRST CLOWN

Here in Denmark, the climate's unkind!

HAMLET

And how long does it take for a dead man to rot?

FIRST CLOWN

About eight or nine years; it depends on the spot.

This skull has had twenty-three years to fester.

HAMLET

Who was it?

FIRST CLOWN

Poor Yorick, the king's old court jester.

HAMLET
This skull here?

FIRST CLOWN
    Yes, that's the one.

HAMLET
Let's have a look. I'll get in the sun.

                  [Takes the skull]

Alas, poor Yorick! I knew him well.
He always had a tale to tell.
A joke, a song, some merry quips.
And now he's a skull! Oh where are those lips
That would smile at me and sing me a song?
Our life is short, our death is long.
Horatio, tell me.

HORATIO
    Anything, say

HAMLET
Was Caesar like this when he passed away?

HORATIO
He looked and smelt like that, I trust.

HAMLET

                  [Puts down the skull]

Ashes to ashes, dust to dust,
From dust to mud, from mud to clay,
From clay to bricks, then bricks we lay.

It's a thought that inspires almost no hope at all.

That Imperious Caeser now lies in a wall.

[Enter Priest in procession with the Corpse of OPHELIA,
LAERTES and Mourners following including KING
CLAUDIUS, QUEEN GERTRUDE. The corpse of OPHELIA is
placed in the grave.]

The King and the Queen. I wonder who died?

With so few mourners, is it suicide?

This company's fancy and despite the shock,

The body must come from royal stock.

[Retiring with HORATIO to peek on the royal party]

LAERTES

[To the Priest] That wasn't a service, it was more like a
ditty!

HAMLET

That is Laertes, back in the city.

LAERTES

Is there nothing else that you can say?

PRIEST

I'd say nothing at all if I'd had it my way.

But the King and the Queen demanded a service

And a grave near the church, which makes me most
nervous.

We should have just piled rocks on her,

Not laid her out as though she was pure!

LAERTES
So you'll say no more? No even one psalm?

PRIEST
It would greatly upset this graveyard's calm!

LAERTES
My sister'll be an angel while you'll be in hell!

QUEEN GERTRUDE
Flowers for my flower, my dearest, farewell!

HAMLET
Could it be Ophelia?

HORATIO
    It is, for sure.

QUEEN GERTRUDE
[Scattering flowers] You should have been my
    daughter-in-law!
These petals I throw were meant for your wedding,
Not for your grave, your afterlife's bedding!

LAERTES
Oh curse the man that drove you to this.
Once more I need to hug you, my sis.

[Leaps into the grave]

Now pile on the dirt and do not skimp!
Make it higher than mount Olymp!

HAMLET

[Advancing] Whose is the grief that darkens the sky,
That dims the stars?

[Leaps into the grave]

LAERTES

Hamlet!

HAMLET

'Tis I!

LAERTES

The devil take your soul to hell!

[Grappling with him]

HAMLET

And may he take yours there as well!

KING CLAUDIUS

Pull them apart!

QUEEN GERTRUDE

Hamlet, my son

ALL

Gentlemen,

HORATIO

Now this is done!

[The Attendants part them, and they come out of the grave.]

HAMLET

I'd fight for her eternally.

LAERTES

No one loved her more than me.

HAMLET

I loved her more than a million brothers,

Ten thousand dads, and hundreds of mothers.

Following here what did occur?

What are you going to do for her?

KING CLAUDIUS

[pointing at HAMLET] He's a crazy man!

QUEEN GERTRUDE

   [To KING CLAUDIUS] Be patient you!

HAMLET

[To LAERTES] Tell me sir, what you would do?

Would you weep? Would you fast? Would you crawl for a
   mile?

Drink vinegar? Eat a crocodile?

I'd do all that while you rant and you rave.

You'd thought you'd outdo me when you jumped in her
   grave?

I'd be buried with her, and our burial mound

Would make Mount Olympus look just like flattened
   ground.

It would scrape the edge of paradise.

QUEEN GERTRUDE

[To HAMLET] Your ranting, dear, it's not very nice.

Now quickly put your temper at bay!

HAMLET
[To LAERTES] Why do want to treat me this way?
I loved you, but that means nothing to you.
But you are what you are; there is nothing to do.

[HAMLET exits]

KING CLAUDIUS
Horatio, go and make sure he's alright.

[Exit HORATIO]

[To LAERTES] Just be calm and remember our chat from
    last night.
In no time at all, all this will be done.
Gertrude, send guards to watch over your son.
On her grave, a statue we will place
To ever remember Ophelia's grace.
With my plans, we'll have peace in this land before long.
Just trust me. I mean, what else could go wrong?

[Exeunt]

SCENE II.

A hall in the castle

[Enter HAMLET and HORATIO]

HAMLET
Now I believe no time is better
To explain to you what I wrote in that letter.

HORATIO
Of how you returned to Denmark the day
After Claudius had sent you away?

HAMLET
I was lying tied up in my cabin at sea,
When an urge for fresh air did overtake me.
As soon as I struggled up onto the deck,
I found the King's letter and thought, 'What the heck?'
So I opened and read it when I got back to bed.
It was asking the English to cut off my head!

HORATIO
That is shocking!

HAMLET
    It is!

HORATIO

So what happened next?

HAMLET

I picked up a quill and wrote a new text.
'Dear King of England' is how it did start,
But I'll skip to the most important part.
I wrote that 'whoever delivered this letter
Should be killed very soon; on the spot even better'.
I sealed and replaced it when I first had the chance.

HORATIO

So Guildenstern and Rosencrantz,
Your two old friends, you ordered their death?!

HAMLET

I feel no remorse, so don't waste your breath!

HORATIO

What a bloody horror show,
And all because of Claudio!

HAMLET

His letter broke the camel's back.
So now's the time for my attack.
Murdering Claud could bring me a curse.
But letting him live could bring me much worse!

HORATIO

You must do it soon. He will hear of your plan.

HAMLET

There'll be no more delay, I will slaughter the man.

But just as I rage for the death of the King,
For Laertes, I wish that some peace I could bring.
I lost my temper, which was wrong of me.
I should have had some empathy.
Our fates are entwined. He's a story like mine.

HORATIO
Who comes here now?

[Enter OSRIC]

HAMLET
  Please hand me some wine.

OSRIC
Surprise, surprise. It is Osric, sweet prince.

HORATIO
You know this man?

HAMLET
  A long time since.
He's a feeble-headed sycophant,
And that's me being benevolent.
He's got money and land, but not much more.

HORATIO
Sometimes that's enough.

HAMLET
  Of that I am sure!

OSRIC
[Removing his hat] I bring news from the King,

HAMLET
　　Please put on your hat.

OSRIC
But it's so hot, Your Majesty, don't ask me for that.

HAMLET
No, it's not, it's cold today.

OSRIC
Indeed it is! On my head it will stay!

　　　　　[Putting his hat back on]

HAMLET
But it's humid and dry; your head it will ache.

OSRIC
You're right again, sir, your advice I will take.
[Removes his hat] How do I survive when I'm living alone?

HAMLET
What did I tell you? No mind of his own.

　　[HAMLET signals him to put on his hat and he does so]

OSRIC
I have come here to tell you of a new man in court.
His name is Laertes and he's so good at sport.
He is handsome and elegant, fashionably dressed.

He's a Dane back from France.

HAMLET
You are sounding obsessed.

HORATIO
That's quite the glowing reference.

ORSIC
The king wants you and him to fence.
He's bet on you. You should agree.

HAMLET
Then I will act most honourably.

OSRIC
I'll tell the King you like his whim.

HAMLET
And I'm sure that you'll agree with him!

[Exit OSRIC]

HORATIO
What an empty-headed little bore.

HAMLET
He's not alone. In this court there are more.
It's a sign we're corrupt and morally sour,
When people like him have positions of power.

[Enter a Lord]

LORD

His majesty from Orsic received your dispatch

That you've agreed to the fencing match.

He just wants to know if you're ready to go.

HAMLET

That was quick! But I'm ready. Let's put on a show!

LORD

That's such a good thing to hear you say,

Cos the King and Queen are on their way.

HAMLET

Good timing!

LORD

      Indeed, but the Queen has one rule.

To speak nicely with Laertes before starting to duel.

HAMLET

Whatever she wants, she usually gets.

[Exit Lord]

HORATIO

I'm afraid they're going to lose their bets.

HAMLET

I'll use this chance to make my amends.

Laertes and I we used to be friends!

HORATIO

He's supposed to be quite the thing with a blade.

HAMLET
I've been practicing hard and progress I have made.
My skills may leave Laertes reeling.
And yet I have a sinking feeling

HORATIO
Don't say that. You're just going to fence.

HAMLET
I know but I feel an awful sixth sense.

HORATIO
If you want to back out, I'll just tell them you're ill.

HAMLET
I'll never do that. It's all down to God's will.
When our stars are aligned, no one is spared.
The important thing is to be prepared.
The time when we go is decided by fate.
No one dies early and no one dies late!

*[Enter KING CLAUDIUS, QUEEN GERTRUDE,
LAERTES and OSRIC]*

KING CLAUDIUS
Come now, Hamlet, and shake this man's hand.

[KING CLAUDIUS puts LAERTES' hand into HAMLET's.]

HAMLET
[To LAERTES] Pardon me, sir, but my actions weren't
    planned.
I'm asking for your humble concession.

All people here know that I have a possession.
My insanity made your sister blue.
Trust me, I'm a victim too.
Everybody here should know
That my illness is my greatest foe.
I did not once premeditate
The acts which could be read as hate.

LAERTES
My feelings they are satisfied,
Even though my father died,
And my sister. But you're not absolved.
My honour it is unresolved.
By accepting your apology
You would take far too much pride from me.
But I will exchange my love with you,
As I firmly believe that yours is true.

HAMLET
And with all those hidden feelings out,
Let us start this friendly bout.
Give me a foil.

LAERTES
    And mine, if you would.

KING CLAUDIUS
Give them their swords.

HAMLET
    I will make you look good.

LAERTES
Your joke with me it quickly wanes.

HAMLET
Everyone knows you're the best of the Danes.
The King did put his money on me,
But for me to lose, obviously!

KING CLAUDIUS
Laertes is clearly the more skilful chap,
Which is why he's been given a handicap.
By three clear strikes, he needs to win
For my betting slip not to go in the bin.

LAERTES
This sword is too heavy; I will try something lighter.
These things matter to a serious fighter!

HAMLET
Are these swords well balanced?

ORSIC
    They are perfectly stable.

KING CLAUDIUS
Let's lay these goblets on the table.

    [He lays two matching glasses on the table.]

If Hamlet hits in a bout or two,
I will take a drink with you.
He will then receive my army's salute,
And this here pearl I'll put in his flute.

[He places a pearl in HAMLET's glass.]

Now bang the drum and trumpets play.

Let's get this duel underway!

HAMLET
Come on then, sir.

LAERTES
I'm here. On guard

[They fence. HAMLET tags LAERTES with his sword.]

HAMLET
One hit to me.

OSRIC
That was pretty hard.

KING CLAUDIUS
I drink to you; this pearl is thine.

[KING CLAUDIUS drinks from his chalice and offers HAMLET the poisoned one with the pearl inside.]

Here's to thy health.

[KING CLAUDIUS drinks. Trumpets sound and cannon shot off within.]

HAMLET
I'll wait for my wine.

[They fence again. HAMLET again tags LAERTES.]

Another hit. Did you feel that one?

LAERTES
I have to confess.

QUEEN GERTRUDE
Come on, my son!
Take my hanky, dry your sweat.
I may see my son winning yet.

> *[She picks up the cup with the pearl.]*

HAMLET
Good madam!

KING CLAUDIUS
[Warningly] Gertrude, not that brew!

QUEEN GERTRUDE
Will you please stop telling me what to do?

> *[She drinks.]*

KING CLAUDIUS
[Aside] It's the poison'd cup, but it's too late to say.

HAMLET
I won't drink yet; alert I'll stay.

QUEEN GERTRUDE
Come, my dear, let me wipe your face.

LAERTES

> *[To KING CLAUDIUS while HAMLET is distracted
> by QUEEN GERTRUDE.]*

Shall I cut him now, your Grace?

KING CLAUDIUS
Considering things, I think best not.

HAMLET

[Finishing with QUEEN GERTRUDE]
Come Laertes, give me your best shot!

[They fence again.]

OSRIC
There's nothing much in it; they're very well matched.

LAERTES
A hit to me.

[LAERTES wounds HAMLET.]

KING CLAUDIUS
His arm has been scratched.

*[They begin to wrestle, and while doing so accidently
exchange their swords. After they separate
HAMLET wounds LAERTES.]*

QUEEN GERTRUDE
Be careful, you two, before something gets chopped.

LAERTES
Somehow, my lord, our swords have been swapped.

[They wrestle again.]

KING CLAUDIUS
Part them now, they are incensed.

HAMLET
Not likely, mate.
> *[To LAERTES]* Stay here and get fenced!

> *[QUEEN GERTRUDE falls.]*

OSRIC
The Queen she has fallen.

HORATIO
> They both bleed! And they're tired.

OSRIC
How are you, Laertes?

LAERTES
> My plans have backfired!

HAMLET
How is the Queen?

KING CLAUDIUS
> She's not well placed.

QUEEN GERTRUDE
Hamlet, don't drink. Your chalice is laced.

> *[Dies]*

HAMLET
Evil is here; lock the door with the key.
The devil we'll find.

LAERTES
The devil is me!
And you will die too in about half an hour.

[Pointing at the sword HAMLET is now holding]

That's a poisonous sword with a great deal of power.
Before we swapped them, I used it on you.
And now, thanks to you, it is killing me too.
We are now both dead and your mother the same.
Now look to the king because he is to blame.

HAMLET
Let the killing continue!

[Stabs KING CLAUDIUS]

KING CLAUDIUS
Treachery!
No wait, it's just an injury!
That was lucky.

HAMLET
But never again.
Drink this poison, you murderous Dane.

*[HAMLET forces the poison wine down the throat of KING
CLAUDIUS and pushes him on the floor.]*

Join my mother slash auntie down on the floor
With stepdad and uncle, a despicable four.

[KING CLAUDIUS dies next to QUEEN GERTRUDE.]

LAERTES

A final fitting aberration.

That poison was his own creation.

For his death I'm not sorry, but yours I regret.

We may have just seconds, but there's time enough yet.

To exchange our forgiveness for what we have done.

I'll you bear you no grudges, if you bear me none.

[Dies]

HAMLET

Ascend thee freely, blameless you'll go.

I am dying, my friend, Horatio.

All of you watching this terrible crime,

I could tell you some stories if I had some more time,

But death comes quickly to my door.

To be or not is a choice no more.

Horatio, please do this for me;

Report my life judiciously!

HORATIO

So little time and so much death.

Too little chance to catch my breath.

Maybe I should take a drop.

There's still some poison in this cup.

HAMLET

If you love me, let it go!

You're a survivor, Horatio!

If for death you can but wait,

Who will put my story straight?

[Marching with drums heard in the distance]

What warlike noise does this way pass?

OSRIC
From Poland it's Young Fortinbras!
Fresh from victory over the Poles,
He's come to haul us over the coals.
I hope he doesn't embarrass us.
He's with some English ambassadors.

HAMLET
This poison, it distorts my views.
I cannot live to hear their news.
With a final breath, just one more thing.
I think that Fortinbras should be King.
Tell him how it came to this.
It's time to go. I hope it's bliss.

[Dies]

HORATIO
Good night, sweet prince. May the angels appear.
Those drums are much closer.

[March within]

[Enter FORTINBRAS, with the English Ambassadors]

PRINCE FORTINBRAS
    What's going on here?

HORATIO
If you like to see death, I would say you're in luck.

PRINCE FORTINBRAS
This death it is greedy, so many it's struck.

FIRST AMBASSADOR
The sight is so dismal; I've seen quite enough.
And in England we are used to this kind of stuff!
We killed your pair and have come for the thanks.

HORATIO
Guildenstern and Rosencrantz?
Well even if Claud had survived this act,
He wouldn't have thanked you for relaying that fact.
It's just become part of a long, twisted story
That's ended like this, both tragic and gory.

[Pointing to the bodies of the royal family]

Help move these bodies and put them on view.
They play the main roles in the tale I'll tell you,
Of carnal, bloody, and unnatural deeds,
Of casual slaughters, and girls in the weeds,
Of deaths brought by cunning and madness mistook.

FIRST AMBASSADOR
It sounds quite dramatic; it should be a book!

PRINCE FORTINBRAS
But this dark cloud it has a silver lining.
It offers me Denmark, and I'm not declining.

HORATIO

Of that I have some cause to speak.

Hamlet's vision of Denmark, he gave me a peek.

And I'd like, if I may, to share it with you.

When you are crowned King; it's the least I can do.

PRINCE FORTINBRAS

Absolutely. I'm willing to hear.

But first let's get this palace clear.

Place Hamlet front and centre-stage,

The uncrowned King of a fictional age.

Pick up the others, all those that have keeled,

They remind me of a battlefield.

Fire cannons for Hamlet; may he long be remembered,

And I hope that as King I will not be dismembered.

We've had quite enough of these guts and this gore

In the quiet, secluded Elsinore!

[A death march song is played. They all exit, carrying off the dead bodies.]

More Drama Resources from Alphabet Publishing

Silly Shakespeare for Students by Paul Leonard Murray

A Midsummer Night's Dream
Macbeth
Pericles
Hamlet
Othello
Twelfth Night

Short Original Plays by Alice Savage

Just Desserts: A foodie drama about a chef gone bad
Introducing Rob: Lola's family loves her new boyfriend. Until they actually meet him
Colorado Ghost Story: Two exchange students get into trouble in the old West
Strange Medicine: Who decides what the truth is?

The Drama Book: Lesson Plans, Activities, and Scripts for the English Language Classroom: Everything you need to start doing theatre, drama games, or plays in your classroom

ISTD Coursebooks by Alice Savage

The Integrated Skills Through Drama coursebooks contain a complete curriculum built around an original one-act play. Aimed at intermediate learners, teenagers and older.

Her Own Worst Enemy: A serious comedy about choosing a major

Only the Best Intentions: A love triangle between a guy, a girl and a game

Rising Water: A stormy drama about what happens to people in a crisis

Alphabet
PUBLISHING

Alphabet Publishing is an independent publisher of creative and innovative educational material. All of our resources were conceived and created by teachers working in the classroom. We support our creators by giving them creative control and by sharing profits. Learn more about us and our resources at www.alphabetpublish.com

www.ingramcontent.com/pod-product-compliance
Lightning Source LLC
Chambersburg PA
CBHW021639120626
46545CB00002B/626